BASHŌ'S JOURNEY

Bashō's Journey

The Literary Prose of Matsuo Bashō

Translated with an
Introduction by
David Landis Barnhill

STATE UNIVERSITY OF NEW YORK PRESS

Published by
State University of New York Press, Albany

For information, address State University of New York Press,
90 State Street, Suite 700, Albany, NY 12207

Production by Kelli Williams
Marketing by Michael Campochiaro

Library of Congress Cataloging in Publication Data

Matsuo Bashō, 1644–1694.
   Bashō's journey : the literary prose of Matsuo Bashō / translated with an
introduction by David Landis Barnhill.
      p. cm.
   Includes bibliographical references and index.
   Contents: Journey of bleached bones (Nozarashi Kiko) — Kashima journal
(Kashima kiko) — Knapsack notebook (Oi no kobumi) — Sarashina journal
(Sarashina kiko) — The narrow road to the deep north (Oku no hosomichi)
— Saga diary (Saga nikki) — Selected haibun.
   ISBN 0-7914-6413-X (hc. : alk. paper)
   ISBN 0-7914-6414-8 (pbk.: alk. paper)
   1. Matsuo Bashō, 1644–1694—Travel—Japan. 2. Japan—Description and
travel—Early works to 1800. 3. Authors, Japanese—Edo period, 1600–
1868—Travel. I. Barnhill, David Landis. II. Title.
PL794.4.A6 2005
895.6'132—dc22
                                                    2004054047

10 9 8 7 6 5 4 3 2 1

for Chuck and Larry Barnhill
true brothers along the path

CONTENTS

ACKNOWLEDGMENTS   IX

SELECTED CHRONOLOGY OF THE LIFE OF MATSUO BASHŌ   XI

MAPS   XIV

INTRODUCTION: BASHŌ'S JOURNEY   1

1. JOURNEY OF BLEACHED BONES IN A FIELD   13

2. KASHIMA JOURNAL (*KASHIMA KIKŌ*)   23

3. KNAPSACK NOTEBOOK (*OI NO KOBUMI*)   29

4. SARASHINA JOURNAL (*SARASHINA KIKŌ*)   45

5. THE NARROW ROAD TO THE DEEP NORTH
(*OKU NO HOSOMICHI*)   49

6. SAGA DIARY (*SAGA NIKKI*)   79

SELECTED HAIBUN   91

NOTES   145

VII

GLOSSARY 181

BIBLIOGRAPHY 185

INDEX 189

ACKNOWLEDGMENTS

Although Matsuo Bashō (1644–1694) was certainly a great poet, his true genius only unfolds in his literary prose. The great theme in his prose is the journey, a path through nature, time, spiritual reality, and one's life: "Each day is a journey, the journey itself home." This translation has certainly been a journey, decades in the making, with numerous people who have impacted it in a variety of ways. Professor Lee Yearley first introduced me to East Asian culture, the study of religion, and the intellectual life. Poets Kenneth Rexroth and Gary Snyder intensified my interest while enriching my perspective. Professors Edwin Good and Susan Matisoff were instrumental to my graduate work on Bashō, as was Makoto Ueda, whose scholarship on Bashō has been extraordinarily important. Friends Scott, Jerry, Phil, Zack, and Bill helped ensure the trip would be a long and strange one. My wife, enduring my solitary character and obsessive work, has been a true companion along the way. Guilford College provided a nourishing environment for someone dedicated to interdisciplinary approaches to learning, and the University of Wisconsin Oshkosh now serves as a productive home for such wayfaring. Thanks to Daniel Sattler for assiduous work on the maps. And I am grateful to Nancy Ellegate and the State University of New York Press for their support of this project.

SELECTED CHRONOLOGY OF
THE LIFE OF MATSUO BASHŌ

1644   Matsuo Kinsaku (Bashō) is born in Ueno, Iga Province.

1656   Matsuo Yozaemon, Bashō's father, dies.

1662   Earliest extant poem.

1666   Death of Tōdō Yoshitada, Bashō's friend and fellow
        poet, son of his Lord.

1672   Dedicates a poetry contest he judged, *The Seashell
        Game (Kai ōi)*, at a Shinto Shrine. He moves to Edo.

1675   Participates in a linked-verse (*haikai no renga*) gather-
        ing with Nishiyama Sōin (1605–82), the founder of the
        Danrin School. By now he has students, including
        Sugiyama Sanpū (1647–1732) and Takarai Kikaku
        (1661–1707).

1676   Participates in two Danrin-style linked-verse sequences,
        Two Poets in Edo (Edo ryōgin shū).

1677   Begins to work at the waterworks department in Edo
        as he continues to be a rising star in the Danrin
        school.

1679   Becomes a lay monk.

1680   Two major collections by his school are published,
        *Twenty Solo Sequences by Tōsei's Disciples (Tōsei
        montei dokugin nijikkasen)* and *Haikai Contests*

(*Haikai awase*). He moves out of central Edo into a
hut on the rustic outskirts in the Fukagawa district.
His poetry begins to reflect the emotional intensity and
spiritual depth of Chinese poetry.

1681   A disciple transplants a *bashō* (banana) tree at the hut.
       Before the year is over, the hut and the poet are known
       by that name. He practices Zen meditation under
       Butchō (1642–1716), and Zen and Chinese Daoism
       become influential in his poetry.

1683   The Bashō Hut is destroyed by fire in January. The
       first major anthology of his school, *Shriveled Chest-
       nuts* (*Minashiguri*), is published. In August his mother
       dies.

1684   In September, he begins a long journey to the west that
       will give rise to his first travel journal, *Journal of
       Bleached Bones in a Field* (*Nozarashi kikō*). During a
       visit in Nagoya, he leads five linked-verse sequences
       (*kasen*) that will be published as *The Winter Sun*
       (*Fuyu no hi*).

1685   Visits his native village of Ueno to celebrate the New
       Year. After several other stops, he returns to Edo in
       summer, which concludes the *Bleached Bones* journey.

1686   Writes the unfinished *Critical Notes on the New Year
       Sequence* (*Hatsukaishi hyōchū*).

1687   In October, travels to Kashima Shrine to see the har-
       vest moon, which results in *Kashima Journal* (*Kashima
       kikō*). He publishes *Collected Verses* (*Atsumeku*), a
       selection of thirty-four of his hokku. In late November,
       he sets off on a long journey to the west, which results
       in *Knapsack Notebook* (*Oi no kobumi*).

1688   *Knapsack Notebook* journey ends at Suma in May. He
       spends the summer in Kyotō and Nagoya areas with
       friends and disciples. In September, he travels to
       Sarashina village to see the harvest moon, which
       results in *Sarashina Journal* (*Sarashina kikō*), and then
       returns to Edo.

1689   Leaves Edo in May for a very long journey to the
north country and the west coast of Japan, which
becomes the basis for *The Narrow Road to the Deep
North (Oku no hosomichi)*. The journal ends with
Bashō heading to Ise in October.

1690   Spends much of the winter in his native village of
Ueno. He lives from May to August in the "Unreal
Hut" by Lake Biwa, and then moves to his native village of Ueno. He begins to speak of his new poetic
ideal of lightness *(karumi)*.

1691   Spends late May at the "Villa of Fallen Persimmons"
in the hills west of Kyōto, where he writes *Saga Diary
(Saga nikki)*. The linked-verse anthology *Monkey's
Straw Raincoat (Sarumino)* is published. He returns to
Edo in December.

1692   After many relatively quiet months, a new *bashō* hut is
built for him in Edo and he becomes busy again as a
haikai master.

1693   Tōin, a nephew he had looked after for many years,
becomes ill, moves in with Bashō, and dies in April.
Bashō begins to take care of Jutei, a woman with three
children. In August he closes his gate to visitors.

1694   Begins a journey to the southwest in June in poor
health. Two anthologies of his school are published,
The Detached Room (Betsuzashiki) and *A Sack of
Charcoal (Sumidawara)*. On November 28, while in
Osaka, he dies.

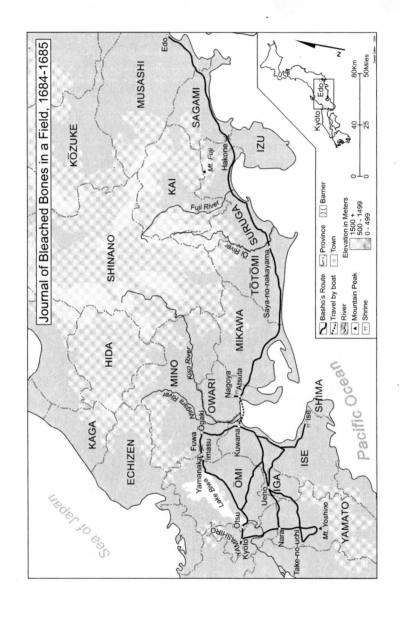

Journal of Bleached Bones in a Field, 1684–1685

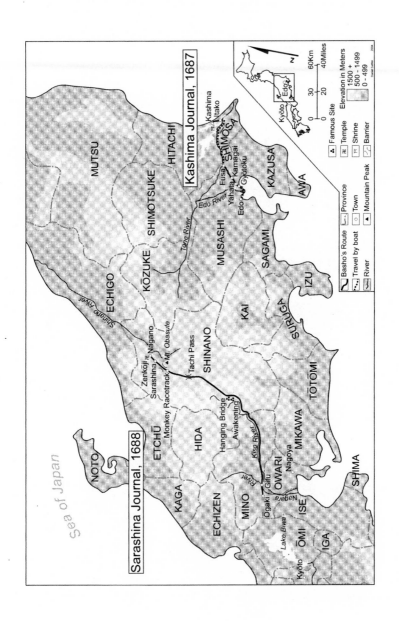

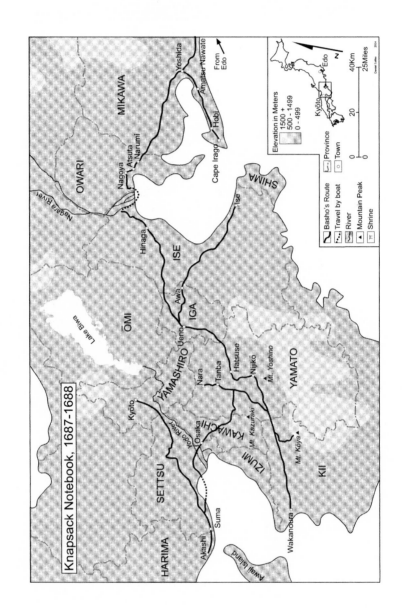

Knapsack Notebook, 1687–1688

Elevation in Meters
- 1500 +
- 500 - 1499
- 0 - 499

Province
Town

Basho's Route
Travel by boat
River
Mountain Peak
Shrine

From Edo

MIKAWA
Yoshida
Amatsu-Nawate
Hobi
Cape Iragō
SHIMA
Narumi
Atsuta
Nagoya
OWARI
Nagara River
Hinaga
Ise
ISE
Awa
IGA
Ueno
YAMASHIRO
ŌMI
Lake Biwa
Nara
Tanba
Hatsuse
Nijikō
Mt. Yoshino
YAMATO
Kyōto
Yodo River
Osaka
KAWACHI
Mt. Kazuraki
IZUMI
Mt. Kōya
KII
SETTSU
Suma
Akashi
Awaji Island
Wakanoura
HARIMA

N

Kyōto
Edo

0   20   40Km
0   25Miles

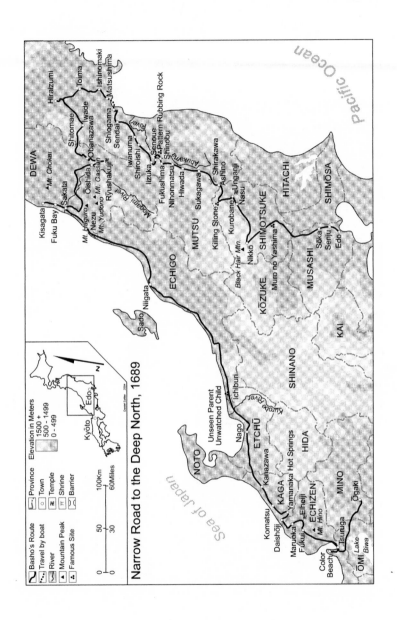

Narrow Road to the Deep North, 1689

INTRODUCTION

I set out on a journey of a thousand leagues, packing no provisions. I leaned on the staff of an ancient who, it is said, entered into nothingness under the midnight moon. It was the first year of Jōkyō, autumn, the eighth moon. As I left my ramshackle hut by the river, the sound of the wind was strangely cold.

> *bleached bones*
> *on my mind, the wind pierces*
> *my body to the heart*
> nozarashi o / kokoro ni kaze no / shimu mi kana
> *—Journal of Bleached Bones in a Field*

In mid-autumn of 1684, the Japanese *haikai*[1] poet Matsuo Bashō set off from Edo (now Tokyo) on a journey. Accompanied by his friend and disciple Chiri, he stopped at his native village of Ueno in Iga Province, where his mother had died the previous year. He also traveled to the Grand Shrine at Ise, the holiest site in Shinto, to Mount Yoshino famous for its natural beauty, and to the ancient cities of Nara and Kyōto.

But his journey was not merely a visit to his old home or to famous scenic spots, it was the beginning of a wayfaring life. He would represent this ideal in five travel journals, the last one, *The Narrow Road to the Deep North (Oku no hosomichi)* being one of the great prose works of Japanese literature. His travels also were an occasion for writing the prose poems known as *haibun*, "haikai prose." In the West, we have become

1

accustomed to thinking of Bashō as a "nature poet," but he was also a great prose stylist, and much of his literary prose is inextricably related to his itinerant life.

This trip lasted until early summer of 1685. One result was *Journal of Bleached Bones in a Field* (*Nozarashi kikō*), his first travel journal. Marked throughout by a deep sensitivity to the impermanence of all things (*mujō-kan*), the journal begins with the passage quoted above in which Bashō imagines himself dead by the roadside. In the first significant episode of the journal, he comes across a baby abandoned by the roadside. He expresses great pity for the child and asks how it could have come to such a fate, then decides "this is simply from heaven" and, after tossing the child some food, leaves it behind as he continues on his journey.[2] Soon afterwards we read a famous poem about his horse suddenly devouring a rose of Sharon blossom, unable to live out even its brief life of one day. Back in his home village, he is presented with strands of his late mother's white hair. Despite all these images of impermanence, there is continuity through time, however, as in the beautiful passage in which he enters Yoshino and communes with poets of old. The journal, which had balanced prose and poetry for much of the text, ends with a series of hokku with only brief headnotes. The journal concludes on a humorous note, with the journey ended but Bashō still trying to remove from his clothes lice he had picked up on his travels.

It is not known when Bashō completed the manuscript of this first journal, but it was published in 1687, the same year as his second, short trip, this time to see the autumn moon at Kashima Shrine. *Kashima Journal* is most significant for the amusing but complex self-image near the beginning. Bashō is accompanied by a rather pretentious monk and a simple lay person who are presented as a bird and a mouse. He then characterizes himself as a bat, someone neither priestly nor worldly but with qualities of both.[3] In this journal there has no integration of poetry and prose throughout the text. It consists rather of an extended prose passage followed by a series of hokku.

Bashō's third journal is *Knapsack Notebook* (*Oi no kobumi*), the title of which refers to a wooden, lacquered backpack (*oi*) worn by priests while traveling. The journal concerns a lengthy trip west from Edo from November 1687 to May

1688, accompanied by his disciple Tokoku. He returns again to his native village Ueno, Ise, and Yoshino, and ventures farther west to Waka Bay, Osaka, Suma, and Akashi, the site of one of Japan's most famous battles. The journal appears to be extensively reworked and yet unfinished. In fact, the opening passage echoes words in the *haibun* "An Account of the Unreal Dwelling" (*Genjūan no ki*) written in 1690 after his last journey to the Deep North; the journal was not published until long after Bashō's death. Except for the final passage, this journal lacks the dark intensity of the early sections of *Journal of Bleached Bones in a Field*. The opening passage of this third journal offers another humorous and disparaging self-portrait, concluding with a declaration of his commitment to a life of art. The second passage (quoted below) is one of his most famous, proclaiming that true art involves following nature's own creativity. Soon follows a notable review of the travel journal genre and his place in it (also quoted below). The journal then turns more narrative, with a number of memorable episodes of life on the road. The work ends with Bashō in melancholy communion with the past as he overlooks the site of the virtual destruction of the Heike clan at Ichinotani at the end of the Heian Period. The centrality of impermanence is restated here in terms of the imperial family being routed at the sea's edge, the glory of the Heian court now lost in the waves of time.

On his return to Edo after the *Knapsack Notebook* journey, he traveled to the village of Sarashina to view the autumn moon, which resulted in another short journal, *Sarashina Journal* (*Sarashina nikki*). It begins with a prose section that recounts disappointment in failing to see the moon at its most beautiful and then ends with a series of hokku. The work is memorable for his account of becoming afraid of falling from his horse as they climb a mountain trail. This passage presents a different type of impermanence: the unceasing imminence of death. Bashō concludes the prose section with praise for the overlooked virtues of rural culture, a theme he develops more fully in his next and final journal.[4]

The Narrow Road to the Deep North (*Oku no hosomichi*) derives from a long and arduous journey Bashō made from Edo to the north of Japan, returning to the Lake Biwa area by way of the western coast. The journal begins with his departure in

late spring of 1689 and ends not with him settling down but
rather setting off again in the autumn, this time to Ise. This
work is one of the masterpieces of Japanese literature. Virtually
every Japanese high school student reads selections from it, and
it probably has been translated more often than any other prose
work in Japanese literature. *The Narrow Road* presents a profound vision of nature, art, and the sacred by a writer at the
peak of his powers. Prose and poetry interweave seamlessly, and
like a linked-verse sequence it has a rhythm that shifts from
weighty to light passages, from deep sorrow to lilting humor,
with an all-embracing humanity and sophisticated spirituality
running throughout. The term *oku* refers to the northern "back-
country" of the main Japanese island of Honshu, and it also
means "deep" in the sense of interior, such as the depths of a
mountain and spiritual depths.

   During an extended stay in the Kyōto area, Bashō wrote his
one and only diary while staying at his disciple Kyorai's small
cottage, called "Fallen Persimmons Villa," in the hills just west
of Kyōto.[5] *Saga Diary* (*Saga nikki*) presents an account of seventeen days there in the summer of 1691. He states that "nothing is as alluring as solitude," and the *Diary* develops his central
aesthetic of *sabi* (loneliness) and *wabi* (aesthetic rusticity).[6] And
yet friends come and go, and Bashō makes two brief excursions.
It was actually a relatively busy though leisurely sojourn. He
muses once again on the transience of life and on the important
theme of dream, and the diary is distinctive in its inclusion of
several Chinese poems.

   Late in 1691, Bashō returned to Edo, where he continued to
write *hokku*, linked verse, and *haibun*. In 1694, hoping to travel
far to the southwest, he left Edo, staying for a while in the
Kyōto area. As he made his way to Osaka he fell seriously ill,
and died there on the 12th day of Tenth Month, November 28,
1694, at the age of fifty.

THE JOURNEY ITSELF HOME

*Months and days are the wayfarers of a hundred gen-
erations, the years too, going and coming, are wander-*

*ers. For those who drift life away on a boat, for those
who meet age leading a horse by the mouth, each day
is a journey, the journey itself home. Among ancients,
too, many died on a journey. And so I too—for how
many years—drawn by a cloud wisp wind, have been
unable to stop thoughts of rambling.*
                    —The Narrow Road to the Deep North

Why was travel so important to Bashō? There were many
reasons. One of them might be put crudely: it was good for
business. Bashō was not just a poet but a poet master with his
own school. One purpose of his journeys was to spread the
word of his style and literary philosophy and gain new disciples.
Bashō journeyed also, of course, in order to visit special scenes
of nature. He sought to experience firsthand beautiful scenes
such as Mount Yoshino, Sarashina, and the pine-clad islands of
Matsushima. In most cases such travels involved visits to *culture*
as well as nature, for these were sites that had been written
about by previous poets. There was a long tradition in Japanese
literature of referring to *utamakura*, places made famous in the
cultural tradition, with specific associations known to most all
readers. Bashō tended to write of places in nature handed down
through literature, giving cultural depth to his experience of
nature.[7]

As such, these journeys into nature and culture were also
journeys into the past as well as a way of making the past present. While Bashō was deeply imbued with a sense of the passage
of time and the impermanence of all things, he wrote often of
the continuity of the past into the present. At one stop in *The
Narrow Road*, he reflects on the vast sweep of time, and what
remains.

*Of places made famous in the poetry since long ago,
many are still handed down to us in verse. But mountains crumble, rivers change course, roadways are
altered, stones are buried in the earth, trees grow old
and are replaced by saplings: time goes by and the
world shifts, and the traces of the past are unstable.
Yet now before this monument, which certainly has*

stood a thousand years, I could see into the hearts of
the ancients. Here is one virtue of the pilgrimage, one
joy of being alive. I forgot the aches of the journey,
and was left with only tears.

But perhaps the fundamental reason for Bashō's journey
was religious. Poetry was not just an art form but also a spiritual path, a Way. For Bashō this included a certain degree of
asceticism. Aesthetic sensibility and spiritual vision were sharp-
ened by the physical hardship and mental discipline that travel
involved. Wayfaring also was traditionally considered a means
to and manifestation of a liberated mind. In Buddhism, our
ignorance and suffering revolves around a deluded view of the
self, which generates desires and attachments. The goal is to
become free of the limitations of the self, remove desires, and
live a life devoid of attachments. One of the principal ways to
cultivate that state and to demonstrate one's achievement of it
was to become a mendicant who leaves the security and stabil-
ity of a home and exposes himself more fully to life's vicissi-
tudes. Although Bashō did not pursue a life of mendicancy in
the sense of being a monk, he attempted to live that ideal in the
journeys he took. In *The Narrow Road*, after spending a sleep-
less night at a miserable inn, he muses on his wayfaring: "My
distant journey remained, I was anxious about my illness, and
yet this was a pilgrimage to far places, a resignation to self-
abandonment and impermanence. Death might come by the
roadside but that is heaven's will."

Bashō also pursued the wayfaring life in order to embody
physically and metaphorically the fundamental character of the
universe. He expressed this view most powerfully in the opening
passage of *The Narrow Road to the Deep North*, cited above at
the beginning of this section. Life is above all a process of
change and all things are travelers. And so, "each day is a journey, the journey itself home." Our fate is uncertain, except that
at some point we shall die along this road, as have those in the
past. To be a wayfarer is to manifest the transience of life, to
expose oneself to uncertainties and difficulties, and to be a
living symbol of the itinerant quality of life itself. In this way
one's life follows the grain of the universe.

BASHŌ AND NATURE

Bashō's vision of nature is central to understanding his prose and poetry. While the title "nature poet" is often ascribed to him, some have claimed that it is inaccurate, because he was principally concerned with either people or some form of "cultured nature."[8] This issue obviously raises the question of what we—and Bashō—mean by "nature." There are numerous definitions of this term, but the West has been informed by two major notions of nature. One we can call "dualistic." In this sense, nature and the natural refer to whatever humans have not manipulated, controlled, or despoiled. Anthills and horse dung are natural; skyscrapers and toxic waste are not. Such a definition obviously assumes a dichotomy between nature and humans, and nature and culture. The other notion of nature is "comprehensive" and is seen, for instance, in the natural sciences. The subject matter of biology, chemistry, geology, and physics is everything in the phenomenal world, and architects of skyscrapers make use of physicists and chemists analyze toxic waste. In this case, the opposite of the natural is not the cultural but the supernatural. In such a view everything humans do would seem to be natural.

The dominant East Asian view of nature tends to be different than either of these. What is natural is what exists according to its true nature. It is an "adverbial" sense of natural, since it refers to a way of being. Humans are fully a part of nature: *essentially* we are natural. However, we have the distinctive ability to act contrary to our nature: *existentially* we usually live unnaturally. We do this by acting on a sense of the personal ego and its desires and will. One of the primary religious goals in East Asia is to act according to one's nature, which (paradoxically to us) requires spiritual cultivation and discipline. In this view, we have neither a separation of humans from nature as in the dualistic view, nor the view that everything humans do is natural as in the comprehensive view of nature. The adverbial view, I think, allows for a more nuanced analysis of the human relationship with nature.

In a similar way, culture is not seen as essentially divorced from nature, although specific cultural activities may diverge from what is natural. Poetry, perhaps the highest art form in East Asia, is at root a natural expression of human feelings, in line with birdsong. Great artists create out of their deepest nature, in concert with the creativity of nature itself. But poetry will be natural only if the creative act arises spontaneously out of authentic feelings and our true nature. Poets who vainly (in both senses of the term) *strive* to create a poem are acting out of their sense of self and its desires, and so their art is not natural. The greatest poet, then, is not only the most cultured, but also the most natural, because to be fully cultured is to follow the processes of nature. It is "barbarians and beasts"—those devoid of culture—that are far from nature.

> *Saigyō's waka, Sōgi's renga, Sesshū's painting, Rikyū's tea ceremony—one thread runs through the artistic Ways. And this aesthetic spirit is to follow the Creative, to be a companion to the turning of the four seasons. Nothing one sees is not a flower, nothing one imagines is not the moon. If what is seen is not a flower, one is like a barbarian; if what is imagined is not a flower, one is like a beast. Depart from the barbarian, break away from the beast, follow the Creative, return to the Creative.*[9]
> —*Knapsack Notebook*

Given the continuity between culture and nature in the Japanese tradition, some students of the Japanese culture have pointed out that usually when their poets sing of nature, it is not "pure" or "wild" nature—in other words, not "real" nature. But this assumes a dichotomy between nature and culture that is foreign to the Japanese (or Chinese). Indeed it is a dichotomy that many contemporary Western nature writers and environmental philosophers are trying to overcome. The notion of a sense of "place," which has become enormously important in geography, nature writing, environmental philosophy, and ecospirituality, is one attempt to speak of the intricate interplay of humans and nature.[10] A "place" in this special sense of the term is precisely a cultured and "storied" place in nature, imbued with human history and meaning.

In the West, the sense of place is usually associated with one's home, particularly somewhere one has lived in for a long time. Shifting this idea into the Japanese context, we can think of *utamakura* as "places" away from home. They are storied not with one's personal life but with literature, with the experiences and expressions of those who have come before. This cultured nature is, for the Japanese, truly nature, not a derivative or shadow of the real thing. Bashō's poetry and travel journals are "nature writing" in this sense of the term, not unlike contemporary nature writers speaking of their sense of place.

Such a view of nature goes beyond our dichotomies of nature and culture, wild and domestic, wilderness and town. It is one of the reasons, I think, that Bashō's writings are so significant to contemporary nature writing and environmental philosophy. His works are just beginning to be recognized as something for us to learn from.

TRAVEL JOURNALS, HAIBUN, AND AMERICAN NATURE WRITING

Among diaries of the road, those of Ki, Chōmei, and the Nun Abutsu are consummate works, bringing to fulfillment the feelings of the journey, while later writers merely imitate their form, lapping their dregs, unable to create anything new. I too fall far short, my pen shallow in wisdom and feeble in talent. "Today rain fell, it cleared at noon. There was a pine tree here, a certain river flowed over there": anyone can record this, but unless there is Huang's distinctiveness and the freshness of Su, it's really not worth writing. And yet the scenes of so many places linger in the heart, and the aching sorrow of a mountain shelter or a hut in a moor become seeds for words and a way to become intimate with wind and clouds. So I've thrown together jottings of places unforgotten. Think of them as the delirium of a drunk or the rambling of one asleep, and listen recklessly.

—Knapsack Notebook

Bashō's travel journals are part of a long tradition in Japan, and travel journals themselves can be considered one type of the larger genre of diary literature (*nikki bungaku*). Starting with *Tosa Diary* (*Tosa nikki* [ca. 935]), written by the poet Ki no Tsurayuki (ca. 872–945) whom Bashō mentions above, the diary was one of the two principal forms of literary prose in Heian and early medieval literature.[11] Although *Tosa Diary* was a travel journal written by a man, most of the early literary diaries were by women and concerned domestic life. But with the beginning of the medieval period in the thirteenth century, travel journals became more common. *A Record of Travel on the Coast Road* (*Kaidōki*, 1223) and *Journey to the Eastern Barrier* (*Tōkan kikō*, 1242), were written by the same unknown author, the latter Bashō attributed to Kamo no Chōmei (1155–1216). These were followed by *The Diary of the Waning Moon* (*Izayoi nikki*, 1280), written by the nun Abutsu concerning her journey to Kamakura.

Along with the general trend in medieval Japanese literature away from court literature to more specifically Buddhist writings, authorship of travel journals shifted from the aristocracy to monk-poets, and thus to males. Sōgi (1421–1502) was a *renga* master whom Bashō particularly favored. Sōgi was also a great travel journalist, author of *A Journey to Shirakawa* (*Shirakawa kikō*, 1468), *A Record of the Road to Tsukushi* (*Tsukushi michi no ki*, 1480), and *The Play of Old Age* (*Oi no susami*, 1479). Bashō's travel journals fit into this tradition.

Haibun, Bashō's other principal form of literary prose, can be considered prose poems. They are characterized by a terse, imagistic style that is justly called "*haikai* prose." In addition, they often include a hokku poem, with the prose and poetry complementing each other. Usually *haibun* are brief, some of them no more than headnotes for the poem. Indeed, Japanese scholars disagree on which of the shorter ones should truly be called *haibun*. Occasionally, the *haibun* are longer, with the famous "An Account of the Unreal Dwelling" over a thousand words in my translation. Some of Bashō's *haibun* are minor masterpieces, but unfortunately they have not received the attention that his poems or travel journals have, and the relatively few translations of some of them are scattered in various anthologies.

This book is the first translation of Bashō's prose to include all five travel journals as well as his *Saga Diary*, and the first to present a large portion of his *haibun*. The importance of his prose is just beginning to be realized in the West, nowhere more so than in American nature writing. Gary Snyder may be the first nature writer influenced by Bashō. His early poetry collection *The Back Country* opens with a brief passage from Cid Corman's highly poetic translation of *The Narrow Road*, and his most recent collection includes American versions of *haibun*. Peter Matthiessen also quotes from *The Narrow Road* in his award-winning book *Snow Leopard*, and he has said that he originally considered structuring that work similarly to *The Narrow Road*. Gretel Ehrlich, who has visited Japan, has written several essays referring to Bashō in her *Islands, The Universe, and Home*. The poet and translator Sam Hamill has written *Bashō's Ghost*, which is structured as a collection of haibun written about his visit to Japan. John Elder's *Following the Brush*, written about his stay in Japan, includes the important essay "Wildness and Walls" in which he compares the view of nature in Japanese culture and Bashō with the American policy of wilderness protection.[12] As Bashō's nature writing becomes more widely known, his influence will continue to grow.

THE TEXTS, THE TRANSLATION, AND TIME

I have generally relied on *Matsuo Bashō shū*, edited by Imoto Nōichi, Hori Nobuo, and Muramatsu Tomotsugu,[13] but I have consulted several others as well, listed in the bibliography. I consulted a number of Japanese and English publications for maps of Bashō's routes, but relied primarily on Nakamura Shunjō's *Bashō Jiten*. For two of the travel journals, I have used titles given by other translators. These strike me as worthy of becoming standard: Hamill's literal and alliterative "Knapsack Notebook" and Yuasa's appropriately metaphorical "Narrow Road to the Deep North." For the important *haibun* "An Account of the Unreal Dwelling" and "Words on Transplanting the *Bashō* Tree," I have translated two different versions. The first one given is generally considered the standard version, but the second one is also a polished and published essay; comparisons between the two versions are illuminating.

The power of Bashō's prose style tends to arise from its strong imagism and incisive brevity. My translation attempts to capture that as much as possible. I have tried to be quite literal, not because I was hoping to produce a dictionary-perfect scholarly translation but because I believe both the literary force and religious meaning are best reproduced that way. Whenever possible I have avoided adding words to explain what Bashō makes implicit or ambiguous. We are at a point culturally that the reader can be expected to be receptive to his style and nuance and that a highly explanatory translation is neither necessary nor desirable. But of course this is a relative ideal, and my success, I am well aware, is quite relative indeed. For more information on Bashō's *hokku* that appear in his prose, see my *Bashō's Haiku: Selected Poems by Matsuo Bashō* (Albany: State University of New York Press, 2004).

I have retained Bashō's references to the lunar calendar, which is important in the Japanese consciousness of nature. The first three lunar months are spring, the next three summer, and so on. The full moon is around the fifteenth of the lunar month. Many of the nature images are traditionally associated with one season, and thus the mention of the moon, say, implies autumn, and the bush warbler spring.[14] This lunar calendar does not match the solar year particularly well, so that their New Year's falls on what we consider a different day each year. The disparity is progressive, so that every few years a "leap month" needs to added.

CHAPTER 1

JOURNAL OF BLEACHED BONES IN A FIELD
NOZARASHI KIKŌ

━━━━━━━━━━━━━━━━━━━━━━━━━━━━━━

I set out on a journey of a thousand leagues, packing no provisions. I leaned on the staff of an ancient who, it is said, entered
into nothingness under the midnight moon. It was the first year
of Jōkyō, autumn, the eighth moon. As I left my ramshackle hut
by the river, the sound of the wind was strangely cold.

> bleached bones
>> on my mind, the wind pierces
>>> my body to the heart
> *nozarashi o / kokoro ni kaze no / shimu mi kana*

> autumn, ten years:
>> now I point to Edo
>>> as the old home
> *aki totose / kaette edo o / sasu kokyō*

On the day I crossed the Barrier, it was raining and all the
mountains were cloud-hidden.

> misty rain,
>> a day with Mount Fuji unseen:
>>> so enchanting
> *kirishigure / fuji o minu hi zo / omoshiroki*

13

A man named Chiri was my companion and aide, and he put himself completely into caring for me. Our hearts are as one, and in friendship he is ever faithful.

> Fukagawa—
>> leaving the *bashō* tree
>> to Mount Fuji's care[1]
> *fukagawa ya / bashō o fuji ni / azukeyuku* (Chiri)[2]

I was walking along the Fuji River when I saw an abandoned child, barely two, weeping pitifully. Had his parents been unable to endure this floating world which is as wave-tossed as these rapids, and so left him here to wait out a life brief as dew? He seemed like a bush clover in autumn's wind that might scatter in the evening or wither in the morning. I tossed him some food from my sleeve and said in passing,

> those who listen for the monkeys:
>> what of this child
>> in the autumn wind?
> *saru o kiku hito / sutego ni aki no / kaze ika ni*

Why did this happen? Were you hated by your father or neglected by your mother? Your father did not hate you, your mother did not neglect you. This simply is from heaven, and you can only grieve over your fate.

The day we were to cross the Ōi River, rains kept falling morning till night.

> a day of autumn rain:
>> in Edo they're counting their fingers
>> about the Ōi River[3]
> *aki no hi no ame / edo ni yubi oran / ōigawa* (Chiri)

A poem on horseback

> roadside rose
>> of sharon: devoured
>> by my horse
> *michinobe no / mukuge wa uma ni / kuwarekeri*

The waning moon shown pale in the sky, the base of the hills was still dark. With my whip dangling from my horse, we crossed many miles before any sound of cockcrow. I rode in a lingering dream as in Du Mu's "Dawn Departure,"[4] then as I arrived at Sayo-no-nakayama I was startled awake.

> dozing on my horse,
>> with dream lingering and moon distant:
>> smoke from a tea fire
>> *uma ni nete / zanmu tsuki tōshi / cha no keburi*

I visited Mutusbaya Fūbaku in Ise, resting my feet for about ten days. As night came on, I worshipped at the Outer Shrine. With shadows draped across the First Torii and sacred lanterns lit here and there, the "pine wind from the high peak"[5] pierced my flesh and struck deep into my heart.

> month's end, no moon:
>> a thousand year cedar
>> embraced by a windstorm
>> *misoka tsuki nashi / chitose no sugi o / daku arashi*

I wear no sword on my hips but dangle an alms wallet from my neck and hold a rosary of eighteen beads in my hand. I resemble a priest, but the dust of the world is on me; I resemble a lay person, but my head is shaven. Although I am no priest, here those with shaven heads are considered to be Buddhist friars, and I was not allowed to go before the shrine.

There's a stream in the lower end of Saigyō Valley. As I gazed at women washing potatoes,

> potato-washing women:
>> were Saigyō here,
>>> he'd compose a waka
>> *imo arau onna / saigyō naraba / uta yoman*

When I stopped at a teashop, a woman named Butterfly asked for a poem referring to her name. She brought me some white silk, and on it I wrote:

> an orchid's scent—
>   its incense perfuming
>   a butterfly's wings
> *ran no ka ya / chō no tsubasa ni / takimono su*

Visiting the thatched hut of a recluse living in tranquillity

> planted ivy
>   and five or six stalks of bamboo
>   in the windstorm
> *tsuta uete / take shigo hon no / arashi kana*

I returned home at the beginning of Ninth Month. The Forgetting Grass by my mother's room had withered with frost, and no trace of it remained. Everything from the past had changed. The temples of my brothers and sisters were white, wrinkles around their eyes. "We're still alive!"—it was all we could say. My older brother opened a relic case and said, "Pay your respects to Mother's white hair. Like Urashima with his jewelled box, your eyebrows have aged."[6] Then, for a time, we all wept.

> should I take it in my hand
>   it would melt in these hot tears:
>   autumn frost
> *te ni toraba kien / namida zo atsuki / aki no shimo*

We continued our pilgrimage into Yamato Province to a place called Take-no-uchi in Katsuge District. This was Chiri's hometown, so we rested our feet for a few days.

> cotton-beating bow—
>   as consoling as a lute
>   deep in the bamboos[7]
> *wata yumi ya / biwa ni nagusamu / take no oku*

Visiting the Taima Temple on Mount Futagami, we saw a pine in the courtyard that must have been a thousand years old, "big enough to hide oxen." Though nonsentient, its connection to the Buddha preserved it from the woodsman's axe.[8] How fortunate, how awesome!

monks, morning glories:
how many died, and reborn;
pine of the dharma
sō asagao / iku shinikaeru / nori no matsu

I wandered alone into the heart of Yoshino. The mountains
were so deep. White clouds lay piled on the peaks, and misty
rain filled the valley. The woodsmens' tiny huts were scattered
all around, and the sound of wood cut to the west echoed on the
east. Temple bells struck to the base of my heart. From of old
many who abandoned the world and entered these mountains
fled into Chinese poetry, took refuge in Japanese verse. Surely
one can call this Mount Lu, like the mountain in Cathay.
At a certain temple lodging, I put up for the night.

beat the fulling block,
make me hear it—
temple wife[9]
kinuta uchite / ware ni kakiseyo ya / bō ga tsuma

The remains of Saigyō's thatched hut is off to the right of
the Inner Temple, reached by pushing a few hundred yards
along a faint woodcutter's path. It faces a steep valley—a stun-
ning view. The "clear trickling water" seems unchanged from of
old, and even now the drops trickle down.

dew trickles down:
in it I would try to wash away
the dust of the floating world[10]
tsuyu tokutoku / kokoromi ni ukiyo / susugabaya

From Yamato I passed through Yamashiro, taking the Ōmi
Road into Mino. Beyond Imasu and Yamanaka lay the grave of
Lady Tokiwa. Moritake of Ise once wrote, "autumn's wind
resembling Lord Yoshitomo," and I had wondered what the
similarity was. Now I too wrote:

Yoshitomo's heart
it does resemble:
autumn wind[11]
yoshitomo no / kokoro ni nitari / aki no kaze

At Fuwa Barrier

> autumn wind—
>> just thickets and fields
>>> at Fuwa Barrier
> *akikaze ya / yabu mo hatake mo / fuwa no seki*

The next night I spent in Ōgaki, the guest of Bokuin. When I set off on my journey from Musashi Plain, I had bleached bones by the roadside on my mind, but now:

> not dead yet
>> at journey's end—
>>> autumn evening
> *shini mo senu / tabine no hate yo / aki no kure*

At Hontō Temple in Kuwana

> winter peonies
>> and plovers, like
>>> cuckoo in snow
> *fuyu botan / chidori yo yuki no / hototogisu*

Weary of sleeping on grass pillow, I went out to the beach in the predawn darkness.

> daybreak—
>> a whitefish, whiteness
>>> one inch
> *akebono ya / shirauo shiroki / koto issun*

I went to Atsuta to worship. The grounds of the shrine were utterly in ruins, the earthen wall collapsed and covered with clumps of weeds. In one place a rope marked the remains of a smaller shrine, in another was a stone with the name of a god now unworshipped. All around, mugwort and longing fern grew wild. Somehow the place drew my heart, more than if it had been splendidly maintained.

> even the fern of longing
>> is withered; buying rice-cakes
>>> at an inn[12]
> *shinobu sae / karete mochi kau / yadori kana*

On the road to Nagoya, I chanted verse.

> a wild poem:
> in winter's winds
>   don't I look
>   just like Chikusai[13]
> *kyōku / kogarashi no / mi wa chikusai ni / nitaru kana*

> grass for my pillow:
>   is a dog too being rained on?
>   night's voices
> *kusa makura / inu mo shigururu ka / yoru no koe*

Walking out to view the snow

> market townsfolk!
>   I'll sell you this hat,
>   a snow umbrella
> *ichibito yo / kono kasa urō / yuki no kasa*

Seeing a traveler

> even a horse:
>   gazing on it on a
>   morning of snow
> *uma o sae / nagamuru yuki no / ashita kana*

Spending a day at the seashore

> the sea darkening,
>   a wild duck's call
>   faintly white
> *umi kurete / kamo no koe / honoka ni shiroshi*

Removing my straw sandals in one place, setting down my staff in another, I kept spending nights on the road as the year drew to a close.

> the year ended,
>   still wearing my bamboo hat
>   and straw sandals
> *toshi kurenu / kasa kite waraji / hakinagara*

Chanting such verse, I spent New Year's at a mountain hut back home.

> Whose son-in-law?
>> bearing fern fronds and rice-cakes
>> this year of the Ox
> *ta ga muko zo / shida ni mochi ou / ushi no toshi*

On the road to Nara

> yes, it's spring—
>> through nameless hills,
>> a faint haze
> *haru nare ya / na mo naki yama no / usugasumi*

Secluded in Second Month Hall

> the water drawing—
>> in the frozen night, the sound
>> of the monks' clogs
> *mizutori ya / kōri no sō no / kutsu no oto*

I went to the capital, visiting Mitsui Shūfū's mountain villa at Narutaki.

Plum Grove

> the plums so white:
>> yesterday did someone steal
>> the cranes?
> *ume shiroshi / kinō ya tsuru o / nusumareshi*

Meeting Priest Ninkō at Saiganji Temple in Fushimi

> onto my robe
>> sprinkle dewdrops from
>> Fushimi's peach blossoms
> *waga kinu ni / fushimi no momo no / shizuku se yo*

Crossing the mountains on the road to Ōtsu

> on a mountain path,
>   somehow so moving:
>   wild violets
> *yamaji kite / naniyara yukashi / sumiregusa*

A view of the lake

> pine of Karasaki:
>   more vague even
>   than the blossoms[14]
> *karasaki no / matsu wa hana yori / oboro nite*

Sitting down for lunch at a traveler's shop

> azaleas all arranged:
>   in their shade, a woman
>   tearing dried cod
> *tsutsuji ikete / sono kage ni hidara / saku onna*

Poem on a journey

> in a field of mustard,
>   with flower-viewing faces:
>   sparrows
> *nabatake ni / hanamigao naru / suzume kana*

At Minakuchi I met a friend I had not seen for twenty years.

> our two lives:
>   between them has lived
>   this blossoming cherry
> *inochi futatsu no / naka ni ikitaru / sakura kana*

A monk from Hiru-ga-kojima in Izu Province, on pilgrimage since last autumn, heard of me and came to Owari to join my journey.

> well now, together
>   let's eat ears of barley:
>   a grass pillow
>   *iza tomo ni / homugi kurawan / kusa makura*

The Abbot of Engakuji, Daiten, had passed away early in First Month. Shaken, I felt as if I was in a dream, and from the road I sent word to Kikaku:

> yearning for the plum,
>   bowing before the deutzia:
>   eyes of tears
>   *ume koite / unohana ogamu / namida kana*

Given to Tokoku

> for the white poppy
>   it tears off its wing:
>   the butterfly's memento
>   *shirageshi ni / hane mogu chō no / katami kana*

Once again I stayed with Tōyō, and as I left for the Eastern Provinces,

> from deep in the
>   peony's pistils, the bee's
>   reluctant parting
>   *botan shibe fukaku / wakeizuru hachi no / nagori kana*

At the end of Fourth Month, I returned to my hut, and as I rested from the weariness of the journey,

> summer robes:
>   still some lice
>   I've yet to pick
>   *natsugoromo / imada shirami o / toritsukusazu*

CHAPTER 2

KASHIMA JOURNAL
KASHIMA KIKŌ

Teishitsu[1] of Kyōto is said to have travelled to view the moon at
Suma Bay and written the following:

> a pine's shade—
> the moon at full
> and Chūnagon[2]
> *matsukage ya / tsuki wa sango ya / chūnagon*

Cherishing the memory of this follower of the poetic spirit, I
resolved to see the moon over the mountains of Kashima Shrine
this autumn. I was accompanied by two men, a masterless
samurai[3] and an itinerant monk. The monk was dressed in
robes black as a crow, with a pouch for sacred objects hanging
from his neck and an image of the Buddha descending the
mountain[4] placed reverently in a portable shrine on his back.
Off he strutted, thumping his staff, alone in the universe, no
barriers between him and the Gateless Gate.[5] I, however, am
neither a monk, nor a man of the world; I could be called a
bat—in between a bird and a mouse.

As if crossing to an island devoid of any birds, we boarded
a boat outside my gate and made our way to a place called
Gyōtoku. Disembarking, we headed off without hiring a horse,
for I hoped to see what strength there might be in my feeble legs.
Each of us was decked out in a cypress hat presented by a
person from Kai Province. After passing by the village called
Yahata, we came upon the expansive fields of Kamagai no

Hara. It's said that in China there is a view that takes in a thousand leagues, and here we too gazed far off into the distance. Mount Tsukba soared into the sky, the two peaks rising side by side. And so also in China there are the Twin Sword Peaks, part of Mount Lu.[6]

> the snow of course
> but even more the purple
> of Tsukuba's skies
> *yuki wa mōsazu / mazu murasaki no / tsukuba kana*

So wrote my disciple Ransetsu.[7] This mountain was immortalized in the words of Prince Yamatotakeru,[8] and the founders of renga employed it to name their art.[9] One simply cannot come to this mountain without composing a *waka* or *hokku*, its beauty is so enchanting.

Bush clover seemed to have been spread around like a brocade, and I thought of Tamenaka[10] who brought these blossoms all the way to Kyōto, carrying them in his luggage as a souvenir. Clearly he had no lack of aesthetic sensitivity. Bellflower, ladyflower, short pampass grass, and miscanthus were growing together in wild disorder, while a stag cried out for his mate—it was a scene of great pathos. The horses, ambling around as they grazed, were also deeply moving.

As day began to darken, we arrived at a place called Fusa near the Tone River. Here fishermen catch salmon in wickerwork traps to sell in the markets of Edo. In early evening we rested inside a fishermen's hut, a night's lodging steeped in the smell of fish.[11] Then, under a resplendent moon in a cloudless sky, we boarded a boat and crossed over to Kashima.

In the early afternon, rain began to fall incessantly. It seemed we had lost any chance of seeing the moon. I heard that the former priest of Konponji Temple was living in seclusion at the foot of the hill, so I sought him out and spent the night there. Like the poet who wrote of entering serene meditation, for a while I felt peace and purity sweep over my heart. With the first flush of dawn, the sky cleared a bit and I woke the priest and we roused the others. The moon's light and the sound of rain: I became absorbed in the deeply moving scene, beyond what any words can tell. It was surely regrettable that I had

come so far to view the full moon without any success. I
thought of that woman who had suffered such distress after she
returned home with no verse on the cuckoo. She became a good
companion in disappointment.

> never changing
> > is the moon's light
> > > in the sky
> the countless views arise
> > in accord with the clouds
> *oriori ni / kawaranu sora no / tsuki kage mo /*
> > *chiji no nagame wa / kumo no ani mani*
> (The priest)

> the moon swift,
> > the branches still holding
> > > the rain
> *tsuki hayashi / kozue wa ame o / mochinagara*

> sleeping at a temple,
> > reverent, with my true face:
> > > moon viewing
> *tera ni nete / makotogao naru / tsukimi kana*

> having slept in the rain,
> > the bamboo returns upright:
> > > moon viewing
> *ame ni nete / take okikaeru / tsukimi kana* (Sora)

> a lonely moon:
> > from the eaves of the temple,
> > > drops of rain
> *tsuki sabishi / dō no nokiba no / ame shizuku* (Sōha)

Before the Shrine

> this pine sprouted
> > in the age of the gods—
> > > so holy an autumn
> *kono matsu no / mibae seshi yo ya / kami no aki*

I would wipe it—
　　on the deity's stone[12]
　　　　moss born dew
nuguwaba ya / ishi no omashi no / koke no tsuyu
(Sōha)

kneeling down—
　　crying out in humility,
　　　　the voice of the stags
hiza oru ya / kashikomari naku / shika no koe (Sora)

The countryside

in the half harvested
　　rice paddies, a crane—
　　　　autumn in the village
karikakeshi / tazura no tsuru ya / sato no aki

in the night fields,
　　I'll help them harvest:
　　　　moon over the village[13]
yoda kari ni / ware yatowaren / sato no tsuki (Sōha)

peasant boy—
　　husking rice, he pauses
　　　　to gaze at the moon
shizu no ko ya / ine surikakete / tsuki o miru

taro leaves—
　　awaiting the moon
　　　　on the village's burnt field[14]
imo no ha ya / tsuki matsu sato no / yakebatake

In a field

my trousers—
　　dyed their color and becoming
　　　　bush clover clothes[15]
momohiki ya / hitohanazuri no / hagigoromo (Sora)

autumn blossoms:
    weary now of eating grass,
        pasturing horses
hana no aki / kusa ni kuiaku / no uma kana (Sora)

field of bush clovers—
    be their shelter for a night:
        mountain dogs
hagi hara ya / hito yo wa yadose / yama no inu

Spending the night at Jijun's[16] on the way home

roost here
    on my dry straw,
        friend sparrows
negura seyo / wara hosu yado no / tomo suzume
(the host)

pregnant with autumn
    this dense cedar hedge
aki o kometaru / kune no sashisugi (the guest)

moonviewing:
    stopping the tugboat
        going upriver
tsuki min to / shiohiki noboru / fune tomete (Sora)

Fourth year of Jōkyō, 25th day of Eighth Month.

CHAPTER 3

KNAPSACK NOTEBOOK
OI NO KOBUMI

Among these hundred bones and nine orifices[1] there is something. For now let's call it "gauze in the wind."[2] Surely we can
say it's thin, torn easily by a breeze. It grew fond of mad
poetry[3] long ago and eventually this became its life work. At
times, it has wearied of the venture and thought of quitting; at
times it has pressed forward, boasting of victories. Battling thus
back and forth, it has never been at rest. For a while it yearned
for worldly success, but poetry thwarted that; for a while it
thought of enlightening its foolishness,[4] but poetry broke that
off. Finally, without talent or skill, it simply follows along this
one line.

Saigyō's waka, Sōgi's renga, Sesshū's painting, Rikyū's tea
ceremony[5]—one thread[6] runs through the artistic Ways. And
this aesthetic spirit is to follow the Creative,[7] to be a companion
to the turning of the four seasons. Nothing one sees is not a
flower, nothing one imagines is not the moon. If what is seen is
not a flower, one is like a barbarian; if what is imagined is not a
flower, one is like a beast. Depart from the barbarian, break
away from the beast, follow the Creative, return to the Creative.

It was the beginning of Godless Month,[8] with sky unsettled
and body like the aimless, windblown leaves.

> "wayfarer"
> will be my name;
> first winter showers
> *tabibito to / waga na yobaren / hatsushigure*

29

sasanqua blossoms again
at each and every lodging
mata sazan ka o / yadoyado ni shite (Chōtarō)

Chōtarō, resident of Iwaki, added this second stanza and treated me to a farewell party at Kikaku's home.

now it's winter;
doubtless you'll return from Yoshino
with the journey's souvenir of spring
toki wa fuyu / yoshino o komen / tabi no tsuto
(Lord Rosen)

This verse was a gracious gift of the Lord Rosen,[9] and with this as a beginning, friends of all kinds and disciples joined in, some offering poems or prose, others money for sandals, revealing their deep feelings. And so I had no need to concern myself with the "three months of provisions." Paper clothing and padded cloak, hat and socks: each person collected something for me, leaving me no worries about the biting cold of frost or snow. Some invited me onto their boats, others gave parties at their villas, still others brought food and drink to my hut, celebrating the journey ahead, regretting the farewell. It almost seemed that someone important was departing—rather extravagant I felt.

Among diaries of the road, those of Ki, Chōmei, and the Nun Abutsu[10] are consummate works, bringing to fulfillment the feelings of the journey, while later writers merely imitate their form, lapping their dregs, unable to create anything new. I too fall far short, my pen shallow in wisdom and feeble in talent. "Today rain fell, it cleared at noon. There was a pine tree here, a certain river flowed over there": anyone can record this, but unless there is Huang's distinctiveness and the freshness of Su,[11] it's really not worth writing. And yet the scenes of so many places linger in the heart, and the aching sorrow of a mountain shelter or a hut in a moor become seeds for words and a way to become intimate with wind and clouds. So I've thrown together jottings of places unforgotten. Think of them as the delerium of a drunk or the rambling of one asleep, and listen recklessly.[12]

Staying over at Narumi

> "gaze into
> the darkness of Star Cape":
> is this the plovers' cry?
> *hoshizaki no / yami o miyo to ya / naku chidori*

I was told that Lord Asukai Masaaki[13] had stayed at this inn and written a poem that he presented to the innkeeper:

> today the capital
> seems even more distant
> here at Narumi Bay
> looking across the vast sea
> that separates me from home
> *kyō wa nao / miyako mo tōku / narumigata /*
> *harukeki umi o / naka ni hedatete* (Masaaki)

So I wrote:

> to the capital,
> half the sky left—
> clouds of snow
> *kyō made wa / mada nakazora ya / yuki no kumo*

I wanted to visit Tokoku[14] who was hiding away in the village of Hobi in Mikawa Province. First I sent for Etsujin,[15] and at Narumi we backtracked about fifty miles and spent the night in Yoshida.

> so cold and yet
> a night sleeping together:
> so delightful
> *samukeredo / futari neru yo zo / tanomoshiki*

At Amatsu Nawate I came upon a narrow path through rice fields, with freezing winds whipping off the sea.

> winter sun—
> frozen on horseback,
> my shadow
> *fuyu no hi ya / bashō ni kōru / kageboshi*

Cape Irago is about one league from Hobi. It is the tip of a promontory that reaches out from the province of Mikawa and is separated from Ise by the sea, yet for some reason it was included in the *Man'yōshu* as one of the famous places of Ise. Out on a sandspit I gathered *go* stones.[16] Perhaps these are the well-known white pebbles of Irago. The mountain called Honeyama is where hawks are often captured. They migrate over first at the shore of the southern sea, I'm told. Just as I was recalling how ancient verse sung of the hawks of Irago, I was deeply moved to discover

> a lone hawk:
>> finding it brings such joy
>>> at Cape Irago
>> *taka hitotsu / mitsukete ureshi / iragosaki*

Atsuta Shrine after reconstruction

> polished new,
>> the sacred mirror too is clear:
>>> blossoms of snow
>> *togi naosu / kagami mo kiyoshi / yuki no hana*

I was greeted by people of the Nagoya area and for a while gave my weary body a rest.

> Hakone Barrier:
>> someone seems to be crossing it
>>> this morning of snow
>> *hakone kosu / hito mo arurashi / kesa no yuki*

At someone's gathering

> smoothing it out,
>> I'm off to snowviewing:
>>> my paper robe
>> *tametsukete / yukimi ni makaru / kamiko kana*

> hey, let's go
>> snowviewing till we
>>> all fall down
>> *iza yukamu / yukimi ni korobu / tokoro made*

At the party of a certain person

> searching out the plum fragrance
> I gaze up at the eaves
> of the warehouse
> *ka o saguru / ume ni kura miru / nokiba kana*

Various literary men from Ōgaki and Gifu in Mino Province came to visit, and we composed a number of eighteen and thirty-six stanza linked verse.

After the 10th of Twelfth Month, I decided to leave Nagoya for my native village.

> resting on my journey,
> I watch the year-end housecleaning
> of the floating world
> *tabine shite / mishi ya ukiyo no / susu harai*

I rented a horse at the village of Hinaga—mentioned in the poem "From Kuwana I came with nothing to eat. . . ."[17]—so I could ride up Walking-stick Hill. But my pack-saddle overturned and I was thrown from the horse.

> if only I had walked
> Walking-stick Hill:
> falling from my horse
> *kachi naraba / tsue-tsuki-zaka o / rakuba kana*

Written while exhausted and vexed, it was only later that I realized that this hokku does not include a season word.

> my native home—
> weeping over my umbilical cord
> at year's end
> *furusato ya / heso no o ni naku / toshi no kure*

On New Year's Eve, reluctant to part with the passing year, I drank deep into the night, and then slept through New Year's morning.

on the *second* day
    I won't fail:
        flowering spring
futsuka ni mo / nukari wa seji na / hana no haru

Early spring

spring has risen
    only nine days now and
        these fields and mountains!
haru tachite / mada kokonoka no / noyama kana

withered grass—
    faint heat waves
        one or two inches high
kareshiba ya / yaya kagerō no / ichi ni-sun

In the village of Awa in Iga Province there are the ancient remains of the temple of Shunjō Shōnin.[18] It was known as the New Great Buddha Temple of Mount Gohō. Now its name alone is the monument of a thousand years. The Main Hall is crumbled, the foundation alone remaining. The priests' quarters have vanished, having turned into fields. The sixteen foot Buddha is buried in green moss, with only the holy face visible, while the image of Priest Shunjō is still intact. With such reminders of that distant time, my tears flowed. The stone lotus pedestal and the platform of the guardian lion were enveloped in mugwort and other vines. The image of withered Sal trees[19] came to my mind.

sixteen foot Buddha:
    heat waves rising
        from the stone base
jōroku ni / kagerō takashi / ishi no ue

so many many
    memories come to mind:
        cherry blossoms
samazama no / koto omoidasu / sakura kana

At Yamada in Ise Province

> from what tree's blossoms
> I know not:
> but such fragrance!
> *nani no ki no / hana to wa shirazu / nioi kana*

> be naked?
> not yet, with second month's
> windstorm[20]
> *hadaka ni wa / mada kisaragi no / arashi kana*

At Bōdai Temple

> of this mountain's
> many sorrows, tell the tales
> old yam diggers
> *kono yama no / kanashisa tsuge yo / tokorohori*

For the Priest Ryū Shōsha

> first I'll ask
> the names of things: these reeds
> with new leaves
> *mono no na o / mazu tou ashi no / wakaba kana*

Meeting with Setsudō, son of Ajiro Minbu

> out from an old plum tree
> grows a young sprout—
> plum blossoms
> *ume no ki ni / nao yadorigi ya / ume no hana*

At a gathering in a grass-thatched hut

> the taro is planted,
> the gate covered with vines'
> new leaves
> *imo uete / kado wa mugura no / wakaba kana*

Within the precincts of the shrine I could not find a single
plum tree. When I asked shrine officials why, I was told that

there was no particular reason, it just turned out there were no plums except one behind the shrine maidens' chambers.

> the shrine maidens:
>   the loveliness of the lone plum here
>   in blossom
> *okorago no / hito moto yukashi / ume no hana*

> inside the shrine's fences—
>   so unexpected this portrait
>   of Buddha entering nirvana
> *kami-gaki ya / omoi-mo-kakezu / nehan-zō*

Just past the middle of Third Month, a yearning for blossoms took hold of me and became my guide along the road, so I resolved to see Yoshino in bloom. Someone I had made arrangements with at Cape Irago came over to meet me at Ise. He wanted to share the sorrows of the road and assist me as my servant, going by the name Mangikumaru.[21] I was charmed by such a boyish name. As we set off we playfully scribbled on our hats: "no abode in Heaven and Earth: two wayfarers."

> the Yoshino cherries
>   I will show you:
>   cypress hat
> *yoshino nite / sakura mishō zo / hinokigasa*

> at Yoshino, I too
>   will show them to you:
>   cypress hat
> *yoshino nite / waga mo mishō zo / hinokigasa*
> (Mangikumaru)

All the paraphernalia of a journey can be such a hindrance, so I discarded most everything, but then sleeping apparel, paper robe, and raincoat, inkstone, brush, and paper, medicine, lunch basket, and so on, wrapping them all up and hoisting them onto my back—legs wobbly and body weak—I felt as if I was being dragged backwards and I barely made any headway at all, feeling nothing but misery.

travel weary,
    just as I finally find lodging—
        wisteria blossoms
kutabirete / yado karu koro ya / fuji no hana

At Hatsuse

spring night—
    someone in retreat, so mysterious
        in a corner of the temple
haru no yo ya / komorido yukashi / dō no sumi

in his high clogs
    a monk too appears:
        a shower of blossoms
ashida haku / sō mo mietari / hana no ame
(Mangikumaru)

Mount Kazuraki

all the more I'd like to see it
    with dawn coming to the blossoms:
        the face of the god[22]
nao mitashi / hana ni akeyuku / kami no kao

Mount Miwa, Tafu Peak, and Hoso Pass, on the road to
Dragon's Gate.

higher than the lark:
    resting in the sky
        at the pass
hibari yori / sora ni yasurau / tōge kana

Dragon's Gate[23]

the blossoms at Dragon Gate—
    a splendid souvenir
        for my drinking friends
ryūmon no / hana ya jōgo no / tsuto ni sen

I'll tell my drinking friends
of these blossoms hanging
over the waterfall
sake nomi ni / kataran kakaru / taki no hana

Nijikō

petal after petal
mountain roses flutter down:
the sound of the rapids[24]
horo to / yamabuki chiru ka / taki no oto

[25]Furu Falls is about two miles deep into the mountains
behind Furu Shrine. Nunobiki Falls is found on the upper
course of Ikuta River in Tsu Province, while Minō Falls of
Yamato Province is on the road to the Kachio Temple.

Cherry blossoms

cherry blossom viewing—
admirable it is to walk
ten or twelve miles a day
sakuragari / kidoku ya hibi ni / go-ri roku-ri

with the sun darkening
on the blossoms, it is lonely—
a false cypress
hi wa hana ni / kurete sabishi ya / asunarō

with a fan
drinking sake in a shadows—
falling cherry blossoms
ōgi nite / sake kumu kage ya / chiru sakura

The moss pure spring

spring rain
flowing down the tree:
the pure spring water[26]
harusame no / koshita ni tsutau / shimizu kana

We stayed in Yoshino for three days, absorbed in scenes of dawn and dusk, the daybreak moon deeply moving, my mind stirred and my heart overflowing. I was captivated by Yoshitsune's poem,[27] I wandered astray from Saigyō's broken-branch path,[28] and Teishitsu's "this! this!"[29] stayed with me. But words would not come and I could only close my mouth—it was so regrettable. I arrived here with poetic ambitions inflated, only to end up disheartened.

Mount Kōya

> for my father and mother
>   I yearn so deeply—
>   a pheasant's cry[30]
> *chichi haha no / shikirini koishi / kiji no koe*

> as blossoms fall
>   I am ashamed of my topknot:
>   the inner temple[31]
> *chiru hana ni / tabusa hazukashi / oku no in*
> (Mangikumaru)

Waka Bay

> departing spring:
>   I've finally caught up with it
>   here at Wakanoura.[32]
> *yuku haru ni / wakanoura nite / oitsukitari*

[33]With my heals hurting like Saigyō's, I recalled his troubled crossing at Tenryū River.[34] So I rented a horse, the story of the outraged holy man in my mind.[35] I gazed upon the skill of the Creative in the beauty of mountains, fields, and coast; I followed the traces of pilgrims freed of attachments; and I pursued the truth of the masters of the aesthetic way. I had abandoned my home and needed no conveniences. My hands empty, I wasn't worried about robbers along the road. Sauntering took the place of a palanquin; a simple meal at night was more satisying than meat. I had no itinerary to inhibit me and there was no set time for morning departures. I had just two wishes for each day: decent lodging at night and sandals that fit my feet—that

was all I required. My feelings shifted with each moment, my moods were made new each day. When I met someone with the slightest aesthetic sensitivity, my joy knew no bounds. Even someone I had despised and dismissed as antiquated and obstinate, when I conversed with him as a companion along some distant road or encountered him in hut overrun with vines, it was like finding a jewel among junk or discovering gold amid mud. To jot down such things and relate them to others is one of the true treasures of the journey.

Clothes-changing day

> removing a one layer
> I carry it over my shoulder:
> clothes-changing day[36]
> *hitotsu nuide / ushiro ni oinu / koromogae*

> departing Yoshino
> I'd love to sell my cotton-padded coat:
> clothes-changing day
> *yoshino idete / nunoko uritashi / koromogae*
> (Mangikumaru)

Worshipping at various temples in Nara on the celebration of the Buddha's birthday, we happened to see a fawn born, a remarkable event given the day.

> Buddha's birthday:
> on this day is born
> a little fawn
> *kanbutsu no / hi ni umareau / kanoko kana*

Priest Ganjin[37] of Shōdaiji Temple endured seventy adversities in his attempts to come to Japan from China. He is said to have lost his sight due to the salt wind blown into his eyes. Worshipping at his sacred image:

> with a young leaf
> I would wipe the tears
> from your eyes
> *wakaba shite / onme no shizuku / nuguwabaya*

Departing from an old friend at Nara

> deer horns
> developing their first branch:
> our separation
> *shika no tsuno / mazu hitofushi no / wakare kana*

At a certain person's house in Osaka

> iris blossoms:
> conversations about them are
> one joy of the journey
> *kakitsubata / kataru mo tabi no / hitotsu kana*

Suma

> the moon is here
> yet there seems an absence:
> summer in Suma
> *tsuki wa aredo / rusu no yō nari / suma no natsu*

> seeing the moon
> yet something is lacking—
> summer in Suma
> *tsuki mite mo / mono tarawazu ya / suma no natsu*

The sky of mid-Fourth Month was still misty and the moon of the brief night was exceptionally lovely. The mountains were dark with young leaves, and at dawn, the time the cuckoo sings, light began to fall upon the sea. The high plain was reddened with waves of wheat, and white poppies were visible among the eaves of the fishers' huts.

> the faces of the fishers
> were seen first—
> poppy flowers
> *ama no kao / mazu miraruru ya / keshi no hana*

This area is divided into East Suma, West Suma, and Coastal Suma. None them appeared to have any special local trade. I had heard of salt-making here in poems such as Yukihira's "gathering seaweed,"[38] but I found no activity like that

now. The people net the *kisugo* fish[39] and lay them out to dry,
but crows swoop in to snatch them away. Despising the birds
for this, fisherman frighten them with bow and arrows—not a
proper part of fishing, I thought. I wondered if the practice was
a lingering effect of being the site of an ancient battle,[40] which
would only increase the sense of sin involved.

Deeply drawn to the past, I decided to scale Tetsukai Peak.
My young guide grumbled and made any number of excuses not
to go, but I coaxed him by saying, "we'll get something to eat at
the teahouse at the foot of the mountain," and he grudgingly
relented. He was about four years younger than that sixteen-
year-old village boy,[41] but he led our ascent of many hundreds
of feet as we crawled our way up the precipitous, twisting route
over the rocks, many times nearly slipping, grabbing hold of
azaleas or ground bamboo to keep from falling, out of breath
and soaked with sweat, then we entered the gateway of the
clouds—thanks to the anxious efforts of our guide.

> is it crying from an arrow
>   from the fishers of Suma?
>   cuckoo
> *suma no ama no / yasaki ni naku ka / hototogisu*

> cuckoo:
>   off where it disappears—
>   a single island
> *hototogisu / kieyuku kata ya / shima hitotsu*

> Temple of Suma—
>   hearing the unblown flute
>   in the deep shade of trees
> *sumadera ya / fukanu fue kiku / koshitayami*

Spending the night at Akashi

> octopus traps—
>   fleeting dreams under
>   summer's moon
> *takotsubo ya / hakanaki yume o / natsu no tsuki*

Isn't it said that "here in Suma it is autumn . . . ?"[42] Certainly the essence of this bay is found in fall. The sorrow and loneliness is beyond words, but I had thought that if it were autumn I'd be able to convey some tiny tip of my feelings— which just shows how oblivious I am to my mind's lack of skill.

As if reaching out a hand, the island of Awaji splits the bay of Suma and the sea of Akashi to the right and left. Du Fu's vista of Wu and Chu[43] to the east and south may have been like this, but a truly learned man would have been able to think of many such resemblances.

On the other side of the mountains is a place called Tai no Hata, said to be the birthplace of Matsukaze and Murasame.[44] A road runs along the ridge toward Tanba. The forbidding names of Hell's Window and Downhill Charge remained from the old times, and looking down from Bell-hanging Pine I could see the Imperial Castle at Ichinotani. The confusion of that day and the tumult of the times[45] rose in my mind, and images gathered before my eyes: the grandmother of the young emperor clutching him in her arms, his legs tangled in his mother's dress, all of them falling into the imperial barge; court ladies of various ranks carrying their personal articles, throwing into the boat lutes and cithers wrapped in cushions and beddings; imperial food spilling into the water, becoming bait for fish; vanity boxes overturning and looking like a fisherman's discarded kelp. The sorrow of a thousand years lingers on this beach. In the sound of the insensate, white waves is deep grief.

CHAPTER 4

SARASHINA JOURNAL
SARASHINA KIKŌ

In the relentless autumn wind my heart grew unsettled, filled with longing to view the moon over Mount Obasute[1] in Sarashina village. My friend Etsujin, also drawn by the wind and clouds, accompanied me. The Kiso Road runs deep into the mountains along preciptous paths, and Kakei,[2] concerned that the journey might be unmanageable for us, sent a servant to attend to us. Both gave their all to the endeavor, but since none of them were experienced in traveling, they were quite unreliable. Things got all confused and turned around, but it certainly made for an interesting trip.

At one point we met a priest about sixty years old, dreary and humorless, his countenance sullen and his body bent by his load, panting rapidly as he struggled along with halting steps. Moved to compassion, my companions bundled together the priest's belongings with what we had been carrying, and threw it all onto the horse and then me on top. Overhead high mountains and strange peaks hung in layers. On my left a great river flowed; below was a precipice that seemed to drop a thousand feet. There was not a single piece of level ground, and unable to settle down in the saddle, I was terrified at every turn, so I dismounted, the servant taking my place.

We passed treacherous places such as Hanging Bridge and the Site of Awakening, as well as Monkey Racetrack and Tachi Pass[3] along the Forty-eight Turnings. The trail wound round as if on a pathway to the clouds. Even on foot I was dizzy and

45

shaken, my legs trembling, yet the servant showed no signs of fear and kept dozing on top of the horse. Many times I thought he surely would fall—I was terrified as I looked up from behind. Gazing upon the sentient beings of this transitory world, the Lord Buddha must feel the same. When we reflect upon the unremitting swiftness of change, we can see why it is said: "the whirlpool of Awa is free of wind and waves."[4]

At night we sought lodging, my mind brimming with the scenes of the day and verses half-composed. I pulled out my brush and ink set and lay on the floor under the lamp, my eyes shut, groaning as I pounded my head. A priest, thinking I was suffering from the travails of traveling, came over to comfort me. He talked on and on about the pilgrimages of his youth, the marvels of Amida Buddha, and all that he considered wondrous—only to keep me from writing anything. But the moonlight he had distracted me from was now shining in through the trees and openings in the wall. From here and there came the sound of bird clappers and the cries of those chasing deer. It was a moment that brought to fulfillment the very heart of autumn sorrow.[5]

"Hey," I said to everyone, "let's have a drink on this moonviewing festival," and wine cups were brought out. They seemed rather large and unrefined, their gold lacquer work quite crude. The cultured elite from the capital would think them tasteless, they wouldn't even deign to touch them, but I was surprisingly delighted, as if they were jasper bowls or jeweled cups,[6] coming as they did from this place.

> its inside I'd like
>   to line with lacquer:
>   moon at the inn
> *ano naka ni / makie kakitashi / yado no tsuki*

> the hanging bridge—
>   grasping for dear life,
>   ivy vines
> *kakehashi ya / inochi o karamu / tsuta katsura*

high hanging bridge—
   what first comes to mind
      is the Meeting with the Horses[7]
kakehashi ya / mazu omoiizu / koma mukae

the mist cleared,
   on this hanging bridge
      you dare not even blink
kiri harete / kakehashi wa me mo / fusagarezu
(Etsujin)

Mount Obasute

her face—
   an old woman weeping alone:
      moon as companion
omokage ya / oba hitori naku / tsuki no tomo

moon of the sixteenth
   and still I linger here
      near Sarashina
izayoi mo / mada sarashina no / kōri kana

Sarashina—
   moonviewing three nights
      without a cloud
sarashina ya / miyosa no tsukimi / kumo mo nashi
(Etsujin)

trembling, teetering,
   now even more dew-like—
      lady flowers
hyoro hyoro to / nao tsuyukeshi ya / ominaeshi

biting deep within,
   the pungent radish:
      autumn wind
mi ni shimite / daikon karashi / aki no kaze

chestnuts of Kiso:
　　for those of the floating world,
　　　　my souvenir
kiso no tochi / ukiyo no hito no / miyage kana

seeing friends off,
　　departing from them, and now:
　　　　autumn in Kiso
okuraretsu / wakaretsu hate wa / kiso no aki

Zenkōji Temple

　　the moon's light –
　　　　four gates, four sects
　　　　　　yet only one
　　tsuki kage ya / shimon shishū mo / tada hitotsu

　　blowing away
　　　　the rocks: Asama's
　　　　　　autumn windstorm
　　fukitobasu / ishi wa asama no / nowaki kana

CHAPTER 5

THE NARROW ROAD TO THE DEEP NORTH
OKU NO HOSOMICHI

Months and days are the wayfarers of a hundred generations, the years too, going and coming, are wanderers.[1] For those who drift life away on a boat, for those who meet age leading a horse by the mouth, each day is a journey, the journey itself home. Among Ancients, too, many died on a journey. And so I too— for how many years—drawn by a cloud wisp wind, have been unable to stop thoughts of rambling. I roamed the coast, then last fall brushed cobwebs off my river hut. The year too gradually passed, and with a sky of spring's rising mist came thoughts of crossing the Shirakawa Barrier. Possessed by the spirits of roving which wrenched the heart, beckoned by Dōsojin,[2] unable to settle hand on anything, I mended a tear in my pants, replaced a cord in my hat, burned my shins with moxa, and then with the moon of Matsushima rising in my mind, I handed on my hut to another and moved to Sanpū's[3] cottage.

> a grass hut too
> has a season of moving:
> a doll's house[4]
> *kusa no to mo / sumikawaru yo zo / hina no ie*

I set this and the rest of the first eight links[5] on the pillar of the hut.

49

27th day of Yayoi:[6] the daybreak sky was hazy, the light of
the dawn moon fading and Fuji's peak faint in the distance. The
crowns of cherry blossoms at Ueno and Yanaka—heart torn with
wondering, when might they be seen again? All my friends gathered the night before and joined us on the boat so they could see
us off. As we landed at a place called Senju, thoughts of the three
thousand leagues before me dammed up in my heart, and at the
crossroads of unreality, tears of departure flowed.

> departing spring—
>   birds cry, in the fishes'
>   eyes are tears
> *yuku haru ya / tori naki uo no / me wa namida*

So my inkset began, but I could barely push forward on the
journey ahead. People lined the road behind, watching until our
backs were mere shadow.

This year—the second of Genroku?—a determination arose
to take up a distant pilgrimage to the Deep North. "The sorrow
of white hair piles up under the skies of Wu,"[7] yet there were
places ears had heard of but eyes had not seen—would I return
alive, everything hanging on an uncertain future—and that
night we finally made it the post town of Sōka. The pack strain-
ing my scrawny shoulders hurt most. I had planned to set forth
with body alone, but paper clothing for night's chill, a light
summer robe, raingear, some brush and ink, and those farewell
gifts so hard to refuse: they were all too difficult to discard,
inevitable burdens of the road.

We paid homage at Muro no Yashima.[8] Sora, my fellow
pilgrim, said, "The deity here is called Princess of the Blossoming Trees, the same as at Mount Fuji.[9] To prove herself, she
entered a doorless chamber and set fire to it, giving birth to
Prince Born Out of Fire.[10] So the place is called Doorless Cal-
dron. And that's why poetry about it usually mentions
smoke."[11] Also the fish *konoshiro*[12] is prohibited here. The
shrine's legends are well known.

The 30th: stopped over at the foot of Mount Nikkō.[13] The
innkeeper said, "My name's Buddha Gozaemon. My principle is
to be honest in all things—that's why people call me that. So
make yourself at home and rest up, even if it's just for a night."

What sort of Buddha is this, appearing in a mean and muddy world to aid beggar-monk pilgrims like us? I observed him closely: free of cleverness or calculation,[14] he was a man of unswerving honesty. It's said: "One of sturdy character and steadfast sincerity approaches true humanity."[15] And this man's natural purity of heart is admirable indeed.

1st day of Deutzia Month:[16] worshiped at the sacred mountain. In ancient times the mountain's name was written *Nikō*, Twice Ravaged Mountain,[17] but when Great Master Kūkai founded a temple here, he changed the name to *Nikkō*, Light of the Sun. Perhaps he saw a thousand years into the future, for now the radiance of this mountain shines throughout the heavens, its blessings extending through the eight directions, the Four Classes[18] secure and at peace. And still more—but it's all so awesome, I can only lay aside my brush.

> so holy:
> green leaves, young leaves,
> in sun's light
> *ara tōto / aoba wakaba no / hi no hikari*

Black Hair Mountain was hung with haze, still white with some snow.

> head shaven,
> at Black Hair Mountain
> changing clothes[19]
> *sorisutete / kurokamiyama ni / koromogae* (Sora)

Sora is from the Kawai family, his given name Sōgorō. His hut stood next to my eaves by the lower leaves of the *bashō*[20] tree, and he assisted me with firewood and water. Overjoyed at the prospect of seeing Matsushima and Kisagata[21] with me this trip, and wanting to help me through the hardships of the road, at daybreak of departure he shaved his head, put on ink black robes, and changed the characters used for his name to those meaning "spiritual enlightenment." And so his poem on Black Hair Mountain. The words "changing clothes" hold great power.

We climbed about a half a league up the mountain, and there was the waterfall. Water surged out of a rocky cavern near the ridge and dropped a hundred feet into an azure pool dotted with a thousand stones. Sidling into the overhang, one views the waterfall from behind, so it's known as Back View Falls.

> for a while
> secluded at a waterfall—
> start of the summer retreat[22]
> *shibaraku wa / taki ni komoru ya / ge no hajime*

I knew someone in a place called Kurobane in Nasu, and I decided to take a short cut from Nikkō straight across the broad plain. We happened to notice a village in the distance as rain began to fall and the sun set. Lodging for a night at a farmer's house, at daybreak we headed off again over the plain. A horse stood grazing in a field. We sought assistance from a man cutting grass and though he was a rustic, he was not without compassion. "Hmm, let's see here. The plain is criss-crossed with trails and somebody unfamiliar with the right way is bound to get lost—that's a real problem—say, why don't you take this horse as far as he'll go and just send him back," and he lent us the horse. Two children came running along behind the horse. One was little girl named Kasane, a truly elegant name I'd never heard before.

> "Kasane"—
> must be a name for
> a double-petalled pink[23]
> *kasane to wa / yaenadeshiko no / na narubeshi* (Sora)

Soon we made it to a village, and tying some money to the saddle, I sent the horse back.

We visited a man named Jōbōji,[24] the overseer of the Kurobane Manor. Surprised, delighted, he talked with us day and night. His younger brother Tōsui came over morning and evening and took us to his house, and his relatives invited us over as well. So the days went by. One day we wandered in the outskirts of town. We viewed the remains of the dog shooting grounds[25] and pushed our way through the bamboo grove to the old tomb of Lady Tamamo.[26] From there we went to pay our respects at the Hachiman Shrine. We were especially moved to hear that it was at this shrine that Yoichi,[27] before he shot at the fan, prayed, "Above all Hachiman, clan deity of this province." As darkness fell, we returned to Tosui's house.

There's a temple for mountain ascetics called Kōmyō. We were invited there and worshipped in the Hall of the Ascetic.[28]

> in the summer mountains
>   praying before the clogs:
>   setting off[29]
> *natsu yama ni / ashida o ogamu / kadode kana*

Deep within Unganji Temple is the site of the mountain hermitage of Priest Butchō.[30]

> A grass-thatched hut
>   less than five feet square:
> regrettable indeed
>   to build even this—
>   if only there were no rains
> *tate yoko no / goshaku ni taranu / kusa no io /*
> *musubu mo kuyashi / ame nakariseba* (Butchō)

He told me once—how long ago was it?—that he scribbled this verse on a rock here using pine charcoal. Yearning to see the remains of the hut, I drew my staff toward Unganji Temple. Some people joined us, inviting still others, many of them young, chatting along the way, and before we knew it we reached the foot of the mountain. And such deep mountains: a path through the valley stretching into the distance, pines and cedars dark, moss dripping, the skies of Deutzia Month still cold. At a place where we could take in all the Ten Views,[31] we crossed over the bridge and entered the main gate.

Wondering where the site was, we clammered up the mountain behind the temple, and there it was, a tiny hut atop a boulder and built onto a cave. It seemed like Zen Master Miao's Barrier of Death or monk Fayun's Stone Chamber.[32]

> even woodpeckers
>   don't damage this hut:
>   summer grove
> *kitsutsuki mo / io wa yaburazu / natsu kodachi*

an impromptu verse I left on a pillar of the hut.

From there we headed for the "Killing Stone."[33] The deputy of the castle sent me off with a horse. The groom leading the way asked, "Could you please write me a poem on a card?" "Such a refined request," I thought.

> across the plain,
>   turn my horse over there!
>   cuckoo
> *no o yoko ni / uma hikimuke yo / hototogisu*

The Killing Stone stands in the shadow of a mountain where a hot spring flows. The poisonous fumes continue unabated. There were so many dead insects—bees, butterflies— that we couldn't even tell the color of the sand.

Also, the "willow where the crystal stream flows"[34] stands on a footpath by a rice field in Ashino village. Several times the district official, someone named Kohō, had said, "I'd love to show you the willow," and I always had wondered where it might be. And now finally I stand in that willow's shade.

> a whole rice paddy
>   planted — I depart
>   from the willow
> *ta ichimai / uete tachisaru / yanagi kana*

Restless days piled one upon another, but as we came to the Shirakawa Barrier, my spirits settled into the journey. I could feel the yearning "to convey somehow my emotions to the capital."[35] One of the Three Barriers,[36] Shirakawa, has drawn the hearts of so many poets. The autumn wind lingered in my ears,[37] and images of crimson leaves floated in my mind, making these green-leaved branches even more moving.[38] All around was the pure white of deutzia blossoms along with the flowers of wild roses—it felt as it we were traversing fields of snow. Kiyosuke[39] has written that long ago someone changed to court robes and corrected his headgear before crossing here.

> adorned with
>   deutzia blooms—formal attire
>   for the barrier
> *unohana o / kazashi ni seki no / haregi kana* (Sora)

And so we passed through the barrier, then crossed the Abukama River. On the left soared the peak of Aizu, to the right lay the villages of Iwaki, Sōma, and Miharu, with a range of mountains forming the border between Hitachi and Shimotsuke provinces. We came to Mirror Marsh, but with the sky overcast, there were no reflections. In the post town of Sukagawa, we visited a man name Tōkyū,[40] who had us stay there four or five days. Right away he asked, "Say, how was it crossing the Shirakawa Barrier?" "Well," I replied, "with all the pains of a long journey, body and mind exhausted, and being enthralled by the views and aching so for the past, I could only throw something together:

> the beginning of all art—
>> in the deep north
>>> a rice-planting song[123]
> *fūryū no / hajime ya oku no / taueuta*

It just would have been a shame to have crossed with nothing." A second and third verse were added, and we ended up making three sets of linked verse.

On the edge of town, a monk who had abandoned the world, dwelled in the shade of a huge chestnut tree. The tranquillity of the scene made me wonder whether "the deep mountains where I gather horse chestnuts"[42] were like this, and I scribbled down these words on a scrap of paper:

> The Chinese written character "chestnut" consists of "tree" and "west," so the chestnut tree is supposed to be related to the Buddha Amida's Western Pureland.[43] They say that throughout his life the Bodhisttva Gyōgi[44] used the wood of this tree for his staff and the pillars of his hut.

> people of the world
>> don't discern these blossoms—
>>> chestnut by the eaves
> *yo no hito no / mitsukenu hana ya / noki no kuri*

We headed off from Tōkyū's house, and after about five leagues, past the post town of Hiwada, we came to the Asaka Hills, close by the road. The countryside here is filled with marshes. The time of cutting *katsumi*[45] was approaching, so I asked people which plant it was, but not a single person knew. Searching through the marshes, I'd ask anyone we'd meet, muttering "*katsumi, katsumi*," until the sun hung on the ridge of the hills. Cutting right at Nihonmatsu, we caught a glimpse of Black Mound Cave, and then stopped for the night at Fukushima.

Next morning we set off for the village of Shinobu,[46] in search of the Pattern Rubbing Rock.[47] We found it in a little hamlet in the shadow of some remote mountain, the rock lying half-buried in the earth. Children from the hamlet came by and told its story. "In the old days it stood way up on the mountain, but visitors kept trampling the grain fields on their way to try it out, so the farmers got real mad, and they shoved it down into the valley, and so now it lies there face down." Might well be true.

> planting seedlings
>   with the hands—ancient patterns
>   from the fern of longing
> *sanae toru / temoto ya mukashi / shinobuzuri*

We crossed the river at Tsukinowa Ford, and emerged at a post town called Senoue. The old ruins of Vice-Chancellor Shōji's mansion were about one-and-a-half leagues away by the hills to the left. We were told they were at Sabana in the village of Iizuka, so we walked around asking where that might be, arriving at some hills called Maruyama. Here was the site of Shōji's residence. People informed us that the ruins of the Great Gate were at the base of the hills—tears beginning to flow—and nearby at an old temple stand the gravestones of the entire family. Among them, the memorials to the two wives[48] were most deeply moving. Women though they were, their valor is known throughout the land, and my sleeves were left wet with tears. The Gravestone of Weeping[49] was not so distant after all.

We entered a temple and requested some tea, discovering that Yoshitsune's sword and Benkei's satchel[50] are preserved here as temple treasures.

satchel and sword, too,
   displayed for Fifth Month:
     carp streamers
oi mo tachi mo / satsuki ni kazare / kaminobori

It was the 1st of Fifth Month.

That night we stopped over at Iizuka. A hot spring is there, and we bathed and rented a room. It was a crude, shabby place, with straw mats covering a dirt floor. There wasn't even a lamp, so we bedded down by the light of the sunken fireplace. Night came, thunder rolled, rain poured down. The roof leaked over our heads and I was harassed by fleas and mosquitoes: I could not sleep. My old illness[51] too cropped up and I almost fainted. Finally the sky of the short summer night began to lighten, and we set off once again. But the night's afflictions stayed with me and my spirits would not rise. We borrowed a horse and headed for the post town of Koori. My distant journey remained, I was anxious about my illness, and yet this was a pilgrimage to far places, a resignation to self-abandonment and impermanence. Death might come by the roadside but that is heaven's will. With those thoughts my spirits recovered a bit, I began to step broadly on my way, and jauntily I passed through the Great Gate at Date.

Passing through the castle towns of Abumizuri and Shiroishi, we entered the district of Kasashima, "Rainhat Island." We asked someone the whereabouts of the grave of Middle Captain Sanetaka[52] and he told us, "Far off, over on the right, those villages you see there at the foot of the mountains: they're called Raincoat Ring and Rainhat Island. The shrine to Dōsojin and the memento miscanthus are still there."[53] With the roads in such terrible shape from summer rains and my body simply exhausted, we ended up passing by, gazing at them from afar. Raincoat Ring and Rainhat Island: the names certainly fit the season.

   Rainhat Island—
     where is it this rainy month
      along muddy roads?
kasashima wa / izuko satsuki no / nukarimichi

We spent the night at Iwanuma.

By the pine of Takekuma,[54] I felt a deep sense of awakening. At the base, the roots divided into two trunks, the ancient form intact. Immediately, the monk Nōin came to mind. In those days a man who had been sent to be the governor of Mutsu cut down the tree and had it used for pilings on the bridge over the Natori River. Probably because of this, Nōin[55] wrote: "There are no traces, now, of a pine." Time and again pines have been cut down and planted, it is said. Now, the image of a thousand years, truly an auspicious tree.

> the Takekuma Pine:
>   show it to him,
>   late-blooming cherries
> *takekuma no / matsu mise mōshimase / osozakura*

Kyohaku gave me this hokku as a farewell gift, so I wrote,

> since the cherries bloomed,
>   I've longed to see this pine: two trunks
>   after three month's passage[56]
> *sakura yori / matsu wa futaki o / mitsukigoshi*

We crossed the Natori River and entered Sendai. It was the day of decking houses[57] with blue irises, and we sought out an inn and stayed four or five days. A painter named Kaemon lives here. I had heard he was a man with some artistic spirit, so I got to know him. "For years I've been searching out famous places that have fallen into obscurity," he said, and he spent a whole day showing us around. The bush clover of the Miyagi Fields were growing prolifically, and I found myself imagining this scene in autumn bloom. At this season, the pieris are in flower at Tamada, Yokono, and Azalea Hill.[58] We came into a pine grove so dense no sunlight could filter in—a place known as "Under the Trees," so we were told. There must have been this kind of heavy dew in the old days as well; it was here that the poet wrote, "Attendants—the umbrella."[59] We offered prayers at the Hall of the Healing Buddha, the Tenjin Shrine,[60] and a few other places, and then day began to darken. Kaemon sent us off with his sketches of Matsushima, Shiogama, and other sites, and for a farewell gift he gave us two pairs of straw sandals, the thongs dyed dark blue. It was a gift that revealed him to be a man truly devoted to the aesthetic way.

> I'll bind blue flags
>   around my feet:
>   sandal cords
> *ayamegusa / ashi ni musuban / waraji no o*

We continued on, following the map given to us, and came upon the Ten Strand Sedge at the foot of the mountains along the Narrow Road to the Deep North. Even today, they say, farmers weave Ten Strand Sedge mats to present to the Governor.

Tsubo Stone Monument
Located at Taga Castle in Ichikawa Village

The Stone Monument of Tsubo, over six feet high and perhaps three feet wide, has an inscription barely visible beneath the moss. It lists the distances to all four corners of the land. "This castle was built in the first year of Jinki (724) by Ōno no Ason Azumahito, Inspector General and Commander of the Garrison. In the sixth year of Tempyō-hōji (762), it was rebuilt by Emi no Ason Asakari, Councilor and Commanding Pacifier of the Eastern Sea and Eastern Mountain Provinces. 1st day of Twelfth Month."[61] So it was during the reign of Emperor Shōmu.[62]

Of places made famous in the poetry since long ago, many are still handed down to us in verse. But mountains crumble, rivers change course, roadways are altered, stones are buried in the earth, trees grow old and are replaced by saplings: time goes by and the world shifts, and the traces of the past are unstable. Yet now before this monument, which certainly has stood a thousand years, I could see into the hearts of the ancients. Here is one virtue of the pilgrimage, one joy of being alive. I forgot the aches of the journey, and was left with only tears.

From there we visited Tama River in Noda and the Offshore Rock. At Sue no Matsuyama, a temple called Masshōzan had been built.[63] The spaces between the pines were filled with graves, and sorrow swept over me at the thought that this was the fate of all the vows of "shared wings and interwoven branches."[64] We heard the vesper bell tolling at Shiogama Bay.

The sky of summer rains cleared a bit, and under the dim evening moon, Magaki Island seemed quite near. Fishing boats rowed in, and at the sound of the men dividing the catch, I could feel the heart of the poet who wrote of "the sadness as they are pulled ashore"[65]—it was so deeply moving. That night a blind ministrel played the *biwa* and chanted something called "ballads of the north country." Neither Heike tales nor ballad dances,[66] these high-pitched countrified tunes sounded strident right by my pillow. Yet it is truly admirable that old customs of a remote land are not forgotten.

Early morning, we paid homage to the Myōjin Shrine in Shiogama. Rebuilt by the governor,[67] its pillars were imposing, its painted rafters resplendent, with step after steep stone step, the morning sun sparkling on the vermillion lacquered fence. Even in this dusty region far at the end of the road, the miraculous spirit of the deities is made manifest—such is the way of our country, precious indeed.

Before the shrine is an ancient splendid lantern. On the metal door is written: "Third Year of Bunji, Presented by Izumi Saburō."[68] Images of five hundred years ago floated before my eyes, and somehow I felt so strange. Izumi was a valiant and righteous warrior, loyal and filial. His fame endures even today; no one does not revere him. Truly it's said, "Practice the Way, maintain righteousness. Fame follows of itself."[69]

Already noon was approaching. We hired a boat and set off for Matsushima.[70] After about two leagues, we arrived at the shore of Ojima. It has been said many times that Matsushima has the most splendid scenery in this wondrous land, in no way inferior to Lake Dongting or West Lake.[71] Opening to the sea in the southeast, the bay is three leagues wide, swelling with the ocean like Zhe River.[72] Here are islands upon islands of limitless number, some towering to the heavens, others prostrate before the waves. Some are doubled together while others are enfolded in three layers. Those to the left are set off from each other; to the right they interconnect. Some islands are carried on the backs of others and some are embraced, like children loved by their grandparents. The pines are deep green, their branches bent in the wind as if spontaneously trained into twisted form. The whole scene has the fathomless beauty of a lady exquisitely arrayed. Is this the work of Ōyamazumi[73] from the age of the gods? The heavenly skill of the Creative:[74] who could fully capture it in painting or in words?

Ojima Island connects to the mainland and extends out to sea. On it are the remains of Zen Master Ungo's[75] hut and his meditation rock. Here and there under the shade of pines are those who have abandoned the world. Smoke from fallen needles and pine cones rise from their grass huts as they dwell in tranquillity. I wondered what kind of people they were and approached with a sense of yearning, when the rising moon became reflected on the sea, transforming the daytime scene. I returned to the shore and sought lodging. I opened the window on the second floor to sleep within the wind and clouds, overcome by a feeling of mystery and wonder.

> Matsushima—
>   borrow the wings of the crane,
>   cuckoo
> *matsushima ya / tsuru ni mi o kare / hototogisu* (Sora)

I gave up trying to write of such beauty and went to bed, but I could not sleep. When I left my old hut in Edo I was given Chinese poems on Matsushima by Sodō and waka on Matsu ga Urashima by Hara Anteki.[76] I opened my pack and took them out, making them my friend through the night, along with hokku of Sanpū and Jokushi.[77]

The 11th: we worshipped at Zuiganji. Thirty-two generations past, Makabe no Heishirō[78] entered the priesthood, journeyed to Tang China, and upon his return founded this temple. Later, by the virtuous work of Zen Master Ungon, the seven tiled-roof halls were rebuilt, shimmering with gold walls and resplendent ornamentations, now a magnificent cathedral, a Buddha Land right here. I yearned to know where the temple of that famous holy man Kembutsu[79] might be.

The 12th: we set off for Hiraizumi by way of such celebrated sites as Aneha Pine and Odae Bridge,[80] taking paths untravelled save for hunters and woodcutters, losing our way, taking a wrong turn, at last coming out at a port town called Ishinomaki. Visible across the sea was Mount Kinka, "where golden flowers bloom,"[81] with hundreds of cargo boats thronging the inlet and houses vying for land, smoke from hearth fires rising. "I sure never intended to end up in a place like this," I thought, and when we sought lodging, no one would lend us a room. Eventually, we passed the night in some miserable shack and at daybreak headed off uncertainly on roads unknown. As we traversed a long river embankment we could glimpse far off Sleeve Crossing, Spotted Tail Pasture, and the Mano Reed Plain. We made our way beside a long and dreary marsh and put up for a night at a place called Toima, then finally made it to Hiraizumi. Distance covered: over twenty leagues I'd guess.

The splendor of three generations[82] is now but a dream; the ruins of the great gate lie one league off. All that remains of Fujiwara Hiderhira's castle are fields and paddies. Only Mount Kinkei retains its form. First we climbed up Takadachi, Yoshitsune's "high fortress," and looking out we saw Kitakami, a large river flowing from Nambu Province. The river Koromo encircles the castle of Izumi Saburo and then below Takadachi it pours into the larger river. Beyond the Koromo Barrier is the ruins of the castle of Hidehira's son Yasuhira, which protected the approach from Nambu; it probably guarded against the Ezo tribesmen. Yoshitsune's retainers took this castle as their fortress; their glory, in a moment, has turned to grass. "A country torn apart, the mountains and rivers remain; in spring, in the ruined castle, the grass is green."[83] I laid out my bamboo hat, and I wept without sense of time.

> summer grass—
>   all that remains
>   of warriors' dreams
> *natsugusa ya / tsuwamonodomo ga / yume no ato*

> in deutzia blossoms
>   Kanefusa[84] can be seen:
>   white hair
> *u no hana ni / kanefusa miyuru / shiraga kana* (Sora)

The two halls I previously had heard of in wonderment were standing open. In the Sutra Hall were the images of the Three Nobles; in the Hall of Light were the coffins of three generations and the Buddhist trinity.[85] By now the Seven Gems should have been scattered, the jeweled doors rent by the wind, the gilded pillars moldered in the frost and snow. The temple should have crumbled and become a vacant field of grass and yet recently it had been enclosed on all four sides, its roof retiled to withstand wind and rain. And so it is, for a while, a monument of a thousand years.

> all the summer rains:
> have they left it untouched?
> Hall of Light
> *samidare no / furinokoshite ya / hikaridō*

Gazing on Nanbu Road far off, we spent the night in the village of Iwade. We passed by Ogurozaki and Mizu no Ojima, and from Narugo Hot Springs we intended to head into Dewa Province across Shitomae[86] Barrier. Few travelers use this road, so the border guards were deeply suspicious, and it was a long time before they allowed us to pass. When we made the crest of a high ridge, the sun was already down. We spotted a border guard's house and sought a night's lodging there. But then heavy rain and wind lashed us for three days, so we holed up in the mountains in a thoroughly cheerless place.

> fleas, lice,
> a horse peeing
> by my pillow
> *nomi shirami / uma no shito suru / makura moto*

Our host said, "From here to Dewa it's high mountains and unmarked trails. Best to get a guide to help you cross." "Sounds good to me," I replied, and we hired someone, a most sturdy young man, curved sword at his side, oak staff in his hand, striding off ahead of us. As we followed behind, I had the sinking feeling that today surely we'd face some danger. And just as our host said, we hiked towering mountains and deep woods. Without even a single bird call, and so dark under the trees and so thick with vegetation, it was like trudging around at night. It felt as if dust were storming down from the edges of clouds.[87] We pushed through bamboo grass, waded across streams, stumbled over rocks, cold sweat pouring, coming out at last in the domain of Mogami. Our guide said, "There's always trouble along this trail. To have made it okay—we sure were lucky," and he headed off smiling. Even though it was all over, those words set my heart pounding.

At Obanazawa we called on a man named Seifū.[88] Though a wealthy merchant, there was nothing vulgar about him. He often traveled to the capital, so he knows what it's like on the road. Keeping us several days, he eased the aches of our long journey and entertained us in myriad ways.

> making coolness
>   my lodging:
>   lying at ease
> *suzushisa o / waga yado ni shite / nemaru nari*

> crawl out here!
>   under the silkworm nursery,
>   the croak of a toad
> *haiide yo / kaiya ga shita no / hiki no koe*

> eye-brow brushes
>   come to mind:
>   safflower blossoms
> *mayuhaki o / omokage ni shite / beni no hana*

> those who tend
>   the silkworms: the appearance
>   of the ancient past
> *kogai suru / hito wa kodai no / sugata kana* (Sora)

In the domain of Yamagata there is a mountain temple called Ryūshaku-ji. Founded by the Great Teacher Jikaku,[89] it is a place of purest serenity. "Be sure at least to get a glimpse of it," others had urged, so at Obanazawa we headed back here, a distance of about seven leagues. The sun had not yet set when we found pilgrim's lodging at the foot of the mountain, then we climbed to the temple at the peak. Boulder upon boulder had piled up to form this mountain, with ancient pines and cypresses, aged stone and soil, and moss smooth as velvet. All the halls at the summit were bolted shut, not a sound anywhere. Climbing around the cliffs, crawling over the boulders, we worshipped at the main Buddha Hall. The scene so beautiful, the deep lonely tranquillity: I could feel my heart turning pure.

> stillness—
>   penetrating the rocks,
>   cicadas' cry
> *shizukasa ya / iwa ni shimiiru / semi no koe*

Hoping to boat down the Mogami River,[90] we waited for fair weather at a place called Ōishida. "The seeds of the old haikai[91] had spilled out here, and we yearn for the unforgotten flower of the past, the simple sound of our reed flute softening our hearts,[92] but we're groping along the path and can't decide between the old way or new," they said, lacking a guide along their road.[93] So I couldn't help completing a scroll of linked verse with them. The art of this journey had come this far.[94]

The Mogami River emerges from the northern mountains, with its upper reaches in Yamagata. Places such as Go Stones and Falcon Rapids[95] present fearsome hazards. Flowing north of Mount Itajiki, it finally spills into the sea at Sakata. The mountains overhang left and right, and a boat is pulled downstream through thick foliage. Probably crafts like this, laden with rice sheaves, were the ones called "riceboats."[96] White Thread Falls shoots down through spaces between green leaves and the Hall of Immortals stands facing the riverbank. With waters swelling, our boat was in real peril.

> gathering all
>   the summer rains, swift
>   Mogami River
> *samidare o / atsumete hayashi / mogamigawa*

3rd of Sixth Month, we climbed Mount Haguro. We called on a man named Zushi Sakichi and had an audience with Holy Teacher Egaku, Acting Abbot. He lodged us at a branch temple in South Valley and showed us deepest consideration.

4th day: a *haikai* gathering at the abbot's quarters.

wonderful that it exists

so grateful—
    perfumed with snow,[97]
      South Valley
arigata ya / yuki o kaorasu / minamidani

The 5th: we worshipped at Gongen. It is not clear in what period lived the shrine's founder, Great Teacher Nōjo. In the *Engi shiki*[98] there is a reference to Satoyama Shrine in Dewa Province. Perhaps the copyist misread *kuro* as *sato*.[99] Perhaps, too, *Haguro* resulted from an omission in writing *Ushū Kuroyama*. The name Dewa, according to the *Fudoki*, comes from the local custom of sending bird feathers in tribute. Haguro, Gassan, and Yudono make the Three Mountains.[100] An affiliate of Tōeizan Kan'ei Temple in Edo, this temple is aglow with the moon of Tendai concentration and insight, and burning ever brighter here is the lamp of the law of total sudden enlightenment. The monks' quarters range roof to roof, and the ascetics are ardent in their austerities. This holy mountain, this sacred land of miraculous power, is held in deep veneration and awe. One can truly say of it: a mountain wondrous, forever flourishing.

The 8th: we climbed Mount Gassan. We put on the paper cords and wrapped our heads with sacred turbans.[101] We were guided by a porter—"man of brawn" they call it—through clouds and mist and mountain air, trekking over ice and snow, the ascent about eight leagues, wondering if we were passing through the great cloud barrier into the very pathways of the sun and moon, then out of breath and body frozen, we made it to the summit as the sun set and the moon appeared. We spread out bamboo grass, made pillows of short bamboo, laid down, and then waited for morning's light. When the sun rose, the clouds now dispersed, we descended toward Yudono.

At the edge of the valley was "the Swordsmith's Hut."[102] It was here that the smith found spiritual waters to purify himself and temper his swords, engraving the finished blades with the name "Gassan"—swords revered throughout the land. Was this the same as the sword forging done at Dragon Spring?[103] Gassan yearned for the ancient days of Gan Jiang and Mo Ye,[104] and I could grasp the depths of his devotion to mastering his Way.

We sat on a rock to rest a moment, and nearby was a cherry tree barely three feet high with buds half open. Buried under a winter of snows, this late blooming cherry had never forgotten the spring—truly poignant. It was like plum blossoms under a scorching sky giving forth their fragrance. I recalled the pathos of Bishop Gyōson's[105] poem, the feelings now even deeper.[106]

As a rule it is forbidden by the ascetics to disclose details of this mountain temple. So I set down my brush; I will not write. We returned to the temple lodgings and at the request of the Abbot wrote on poem cards verses of our pilgrimage to the Three Mountains.

> coolness—
>> the crescent moon faint
>>> over Black Feather Mountain
> *suzushisa ya / hono mikazuki no / haguroyama*

> cloud peaks,
>> how many have crumbled away:
>>> Moon Mountain
> *kumo no mine / ikutsu kuzurete / tsuki no yama*

> at Yudono,
>> forbidden to speak,
>>> my sleeves wet with tears
> *katararenu / yudono ni nurasu / tamoto kana*

> Mount Yudono:
>> on the path of treading coins,[107]
>>> with tears falling
> *yudonoyama / zeni fumu michi no / namida kana*
> (Sora)

We departed Haguro for the castle town of Tsuragaoka, where we were welcomed by a samurai named Nagayama Shigeyuki and together completed a linked verse. Sakichi also had accompanied us. Boarding a riverboat, we headed downstream to Sakata Harbor. There we lodged at the house of a physician, En'an Fugyoku.[108]

Mount Atsumi[109]—
> all the way to Fuku Bay,
> the evening cool
atsumiyama ya / fukuura kakete / yūsuzumi

thrusting the hot sun
> into the sea:
> Mogami River
atsuki hi o / umi ni iretari / mogamigawa

We had experienced spectacular scenes of rivers and mountains, sea and land; now my heart was set on Kisagata. Heading northeast of Sakata harbor, we crossed mountains, followed the shore, plodded over sand—about ten leagues—then as the sun sloped down, a sea wind swirled the sand and rain misted down, obscuring Mount Chōkai.[110] Groping through the dark, I thought that since the rain itself is stirring,[111] the clearing later would surely enchant, and we crammed into a fisher's shanty and waited for the rain to pass.

The next morning the sky was stunningly clear. As the sun rose glistening, we set off on boat around Kisagata bay. First we rowed to Nōin Island and visited the site of Nōin's three years of seclusion. Then we landed on the opposite shore where the old cherry tree remains as a memento to Priest Saigyō, who wrote of fishermen "rowing over blossoms."[112] Right by the water is said to be the grave of Empress Jingū.[113] The temple there is called Kanmanjuji. I had never heard that the Empress had visited here—I wonder how this came to be.

Sitting in the temple's front room, raising the blinds, I took in the whole vast panorama. To the south, Chōkai upheld the heavens, its reflection in the waters. To the west, Muyamuya Barrier cut off the road. Eastward lay an embankment, with a road leading far off to Akita. And to the north was the sea, the waves rolling in at a place called Tide Crossing.

The bay is about a league in width and length, and its appearance suggests Matsushima, but with a difference. Matsushima seems to laugh, while Kisagata looks embittered. Grief piled upon loneliness: this place resembles a spirit in torment.

Kisagata—
    in the rain, Xi Shi asleep,
      silk tree blossoms[114]
kisagata ya / ame ni seishi ga / nebu no hana

The Shallows—
    a crane with legs wet,
      the sea cool
shiogoshi ya / tsuru hagi nurete / umi suzushi

Kisagata—
    what food to eat
      on festival day?
kisagata ya / ryōri nani kuu / kamimatsuri (Sora)

a fisher's hut—
    laying out rain shutters[115]
      for the evening cool
ama no ya ya / toita o shikite / yūsuzumi (Teiji, a
merchant from Mino)

Glimpsing an osprey nest on a rock

have they vowed,
    waves will never wash over it?[116]
      an osprey's nest
nami koenu / chigiri arite ya / misago no su (Sora)

As days of farewell piled up at Sakata, we turned our gaze
to Hokuriku under cloud. My heart ached at the thought of the
vast distance: over 130 leagues from here to the capital of Kaga,
we were told. Crossing the Nezu Barrier, we stepped forth into
the land of Echigo, arriving at last at Ichiburi Barrier in Etchū.
Nine days[117] it took, and with my spirit afflicted by heat and
rain and my illness breaking out, I could not even jot anything
down.

Seventh Month—
    even the sixth night
      is different[118]
fumizuki ya / muika mo tsune no / yo ni wa nizu

> stormy sea—
>> stretching out over Sado,
>> Heaven's River[119]
> *araumi ya / sado ni yokotau / amanogawa*

Today we made our way through the most precarious parts
of the north country, places such as Unseen Parents, Unwatched
Child, Turned-back Dog, Retreating Horse.[120] At night,
exhausted, I sought out a pillow and was near to sleep when I
heard the voices of two young women in the front, one room
away. The voice of an old man mingled with theirs. From what
I could hear they were courtesans from a place called Niigata in
Echigo on their way to worship at the Ise Shrine. The old man
had seen them off as far as this barrier, and they had written letters and brief notes for him to take back to their village in the
morning.

At one point I heard these words: "Cast adrift on the beach
where the white waves break,[121] daughters of the shore, we
have fallen to a wretched life. Each night there are the fleeting
pledges of love; what shameful karma do we carry from our
past days?" On they talked, and I drifted to sleep.

In the morning as we set off, they came pleading to us with
tears falling. "We don't know which way to go on this sorrowful road, we are so worried and upset, could we follow your
footsteps from off in the distance? By the mercy of your robes,
grant us the blessing of your great compassion and we will be
bound to the Buddha." "It's unfortunate," I said, "but we are
always stopping here and there. Just entrust yourself to the way
others are going. Surely the gods will protect you from
harm."[122] With these words we left them behind, but for a time
the pity of their situation would not leave me.

> in the same house
>> prostitutes, too, slept:
>>> bush clover and moon
> *hitotsuya ni / yūjo mo netari / hagi to tsuki*

I recited this to Sora, and he wrote it down.

People speak of the "forty-eight rapids of Kurobe,"[123] and
we did cross countless streams, coming out at a bay called

Nago. At Tako it was not the spring of "waves of wisteria blooms,"[124] but people said we should experience the pathos of early autumn there. When we asked someone the way, he said, "About five leagues from here: follow the shore, then into the mountain recesses over there. Just some old shabby huts of fishermen—doubt if anyone will put you up for a night." Thoroughly intimidated, we headed into the province of Kaga.

> the scent of early rice—
>   cutting through the fields, on the right,
>   the Rough Shore Sea[125]
> *wase no ka ya / wakeiru migi wa / arisoumi*

We crossed Mount Deutzia Blossoms and Kurikara Valley,[126] reaching Kanazawa on the middle day of Seventh Month. There was a merchant named Kasho[127] who traveled here from Ōzaka. We all shared the same lodging. A certain Isshō had become well-known for his devotion to the way of haikai, but last winter he died. His elder brother held a linked-verse gathering as a memorial.

> grave too move!
>   my wailing voice:
>   autumn wind
> *tsuka mo ugoke / waga naku koe wa / aki no kaze*

I was invited to a certain grass hut

> autumn is cool:
>   let each hand set to peeling
>   melons and eggplants
> *aki suzushi / tegoto ni muke ya / uri nasubi*

A song of the road

> so red, red,
>   the sun relentless and yet
>   autumn's wind
> *akaaka to / hi wa tsurenaku mo / aki no kaze*

At a place called Little Pine[128]

> a lovely name—
> Little Pine, where the wind wafts
> over bush clover and miscanthus
> *shiorashiki / na ya komatsu fuku / hagi susuki*

In this area, I visited the Tada Shrine which contains Sanemori's[129] helmet and a piece of his armor brocade. In days of old, it is said, at a time when he still served the Genji clan, these articles were given to him by Lord Yoshitomo.[130] Certainly they were meant for no common warrior: from eye shield to ear flaps there is an engraved arabesque of chrysanthemum inlaid with gold and at the crown is a dragon's head with hoe-shaped crests attached. In the annals of the shrine it is written that after Sanemori's death in battle, Kiso Yoshinaka[131] dedicated these relics to the shrine with a message of prayer, Higuchi no Jiro[132] his emissary. Here they lie before me eyes, just as in the legend.

> so pitiful—
> under the helmet,
> a cricket
> *muzan ya na / kabuto no shita no / kirigirisu*

As we made our way to the Yamanaka Hot Springs, Shirane's peak was visible behind. To our left, at the foot of a mountain, was Kannon Temple. Emperor Kazan,[133] after completing a pilgrimage to the Thirty Three Places, installed an image of the Great Compassionate, Great Sorrowful One,[134] and confered on the place the name of Nata. The name derives from the first characters of Nachi and Tanigumi,[135] it is said. Among various strange rock-forms runs a row of ancient pines; and a tiny thatched-roof temple is built atop a boulder. A land of wondrous beauty.

> whiter than
> the stones of Stone Mountain:[136]
> autumn's wind
> *ishiyama no / ishi yori shiroshi / aki no kaze*

We bathed in the hot springs. It's said that their efficacy is second only to those in Ariake.[137]

> Yamanaka—
>   no need to pluck chrysanthemums:[138]
>   the fragrance of these springs
> *yamanaka ya / kiku wa taoranu / yu no nio*

The Master here, Kumenosuke,[139] was still yet a boy. His father was fond of haikai, and when Teishitsu came here from Kyōto as a young novice, he was put to shame by the father's poetic abilities. After Teishitsu returned to the capital, he became a disciple of Teitoku,[140] eventually becoming respected for his art. When he had become a skilled poet, Teishitsu never accepted payment when he served as a poetry judge in this village. The story's been known for a long time now.

Sora, suffering from stomach trouble, set off ahead of me to Nagashima in Ise Province, where he had relatives. On his departure, he left this with me:

> journeying on and on
>   I may fall and yet
>   a field of bush clover
> *yukiyukite / taorefusu tomo / hagi no hara* (Sora)

The one leaving in grief, the one remaining with deep regret, like two lapwings[141] parting, lost in clouds. So I too:

> from this day forth—
>   the inscription washed away
>   by dew on my hat[142]
> *kyō yori ya / kakitsuke kesan / kasa no tsuyu*

Still in Kaga, I spent the night at a temple called Zenshōji, just outside the castle town of Daishōji. The previous night Sora also stayed at this temple, leaving behind the poem:

> all night long
>   listening to autumn's wind—
>   the mountain behind
> *yomosugara / akikaze kiku ya / ura no yama* (Sora)

Separated by a single night is like being a thousand leagues apart.[143] I too listened to the autumn wind as I lay awake in the monk's quarters. Near daybreak, the sound of sutra chanting rose clear, then the ringing of the gong, and I entered the dining hall. Eager to make it into Echizen Province that day, I hurried out of the hall, but some young monks scurrying down the stairs caught up with me, paper and inkstone in hand. Just then, willow leaves were falling in the garden:

> I would sweep the garden
>   before departing: in the temple,
>   falling willow leaves[226]
> *niwa haite / idebaya tera ni / chiru yanagi*

My travelling sandals already on, I scribbled this down for them as I left.

At the border of Echizen Province, my boat was poled across Yoshizaki Inlet, and I visited the Tide-Cross Pines.[145]

> All night long
>   waves were heaved across
>   by the storm,
> moonlight dripping down
>   among the Tide Cross Pines[146]
> *yomosugara / arashi ni nami o / hakobasete /*
> *tsuki o taretaru / shiogoshi no matsu* (Saigyō)

In this one poem, all the beautiful views here are brought forth. If but one word were added, it would be like appending a useless finger.[147]

At Maruoka was the Abbot of Tenryū Temple, an old friend, so I stopped by. Also, someone named Hokushi had thought to see me off at Kanazawa but ended up accompanying me this far. Not passing any place without attending to its beauty, from time to time he wrote some moving poems. And now, facing departure

> scribbled on,
>   now the fan is torn up:
>   reluctant parting[148]
> *mono kaite / ōgi hikisaku / nagori kana*

I journeyed some one and a half leagues into the mountains to worship at Eiheiji,[149] the temple of Zen Master Dōgen. Shunning the capital, a thousand leagues away, he left his traces deep in these mountains, for quite worthy reasons, it's said.

About three leagues away was Fukui, so after an evening meal I headed off, stepping tentatively along the twilight road. A recluse named Tōsai[150] had been living there for a long time. He had called on me in Edo—when was that? Must have been over ten years ago. He was likely old and frail now, or even dead. When I asked someone about him, I was told he was still alive, living in such and such a place. Hidden away from town was a dilapidated cottage, overgrown with moonflowers and snake gourds, the door covered over with cockscomb and goosefoot.[151] So, this is it, I thought, and knocked on the gate. A woman appeared, looking poor and lonely, and said, "Where've you come from, reverend priest? The master, he went off to see someone in the neighborhood. If you've business with him, look for him there." Apparently his wife. The scene seemed as in a tale from long ago,[152] and soon I came across him, spent two nights at his home, then set off for the harvest moon at Tsuruga Bay. Tōsai accompanied me, bouyantly proclaiming that he'd be my guide, rather comical with his kimono skirts all tucked up.

Slowly, Shirane Peak faded away as Hina Peak came into view. We crossed the Asamuzu Bridge and came upon the reeds of Tamae, their seed heads formed. We made our way through Bush Warbler Barrier across Yunō Pass to Higuchi Castle, then heard the first wild geese of autumn at Mount Return, lodging at Tsuruga Port on the night of the fourteenth. That evening the moon was exceptionally bright. I asked the innkeeper, "Will it be like this tomorrow night?" "Hard to say here in Koshiji whether the next night will be cloudy or clear," he replied, as he offered me some sake.

I went off for night worship at Kei Shrine, the site of Emperor Chūai's[153] tomb. The shrine precincts have great sanctity, with moonlight filtering through pines and white sands spread before the sanctuary like frost. The innkeeper told me, "Long long ago the Second Pilgrim[154] developed a heartfelt aspiration that worshippers could come and go here with no problem, so he himself cut grass, moved earth and stones, and

drained the muddy marsh. That old practice continues unbroken—each Pilgrim carries sand and spreads it before the shrine.
It's called the Pilgrim's Sand-carrying."

> the moon so pure
> on the sand carried here
> by the Pilgrim Priests
> *tsuki kiyoshi / yugyō no moteru / suna no ue*

On the 15th, just as the innkeeper suggested, it rained.

> harvest moon—
> the north country weather
> so uncertain
> *meigetsu ya / hokkoku biyori / sadamenaki*

The 16th, we headed off by boat for Color Beach[155] to
gather the small masuo shells. It's seven leagues across the water.
A man named Ten'ya[156] had meticulously prepared lunch boxes,
sake-filled bamboo bottles, and so forth, and had sent a number
of his servants to accompany us. With a favorable wind, we
arrived in no time. On the shore were a few small fishermen's
hut and a forlorn Hokke temple.[157] There we drank tea and hot
sake, engulfed in the loneliness of the evening.

> loneliness—
> superior even than Suma,
> autumn on this beach[240]
> *sabishisa ya / suma ni kachitaru / hama no aki*   —

> between the waves—
> mingling with tiny shells,
> bits of bush clover blossoms
> *nami no ma ya / kogai ni majiru / hagi no chiri*

I had Tōsai set down an account of the day and left it at the
temple.

Rostū came all the way to Tsuruga to welcome me back
and then accompied me to Mino Province. Our travel eased by
going horseback, we entered Ōgaki. Sora too came from Ise to
meet me and Etsujin hurried in on horseback as we gathered at

Jokō's house. Zensenshi, Keikō and his sons, and other close
friends visited day and night, both rejoicing and comforting
me, as if I had returned from the dead. On the 6th of Ninth
Month, before I could recover from the wearines of the journey, I set off once again by boat to worship during the ritual
rebuilding at Ise.

> like a clam from its shell,
>   setting off for Futami Bay:
>   departing fall[159]
> *hamaguri no / futami ni wakare / yuku aki zo*

CHAPTER 6

SAGA DIARY
SAGA NIKKI

18TH DAY

On the 18th day of Fourth Month, fourth year of Genroku, I journey to Saga and Kyorai's "Villa of Fallen Persimmons." Bonchō accompanies me and stays till evening, then returns to Kyōto. Because I plan to remain a little longer, the paper screens have been repaired, weeds pulled out, and a corner of the house prepared as my bedroom. There's a desk, inkstone, and writing box, as well as a collection of Bo Juyi's poems, *Chinese Poems by Japanese Poets, One Each,*[1] *The Tale of Succession,*[2] *The Tale of Genji, The Tosa Diary,*[3] and *The Pine Needle Collection.*[4] Also, a variety of sweets have been set out in a gold lacquered container with five levels stacked on top of each other and decorated in Chinese style. A bottle of fine sake accompany wine cups. Bedding and food delicacies have been brought over from Kyōto. Nothing is lacking, and forgetting my poverty, I savor the leisurely tranquillity.

19TH DAY

Around the middle of the hour of the horse,[5] we visit Rinsen temple. The Ōi River flows in front, and to the right rises Arashi Mountain, ranging off toward Matsu-no-o village. Coming and going are the countless pilgrims to the Bodhisattva Kokuzō.[6]

Lady Kogō's[7] residence is said to have been in the bamboo grove of Matsu-no-o, but there are three such sites in upper and lower Saga. Which is the real one? Nearby is the Horsehalting Bridge, where Nakakuni is said to have pulled up his horse, so perhaps this is it. Lady Kogō's grave is near a teahouse in the bamboo grove, with a cherry tree planted as the marker. She lived her daily life in brocades and silk but in the end turned into dust amid the underbrush. The old legends came to mind, of the willow Zhaojun village and the blossoms of the shrine of the Goddess Wu.[8]

> grievous junctures—
>   the human fate of becoming
>   a bamboo shoot
> *uki fushi ya / take no ko to naru / hito no hate*

> Arashiyama's
>   bamboo grove so dense—
>   the wind threading through
> *arashiyama / yabu no shigeri ya / kaze no suji*

We return to the Villa of Fallen Persimmons as the sun begins to decline in the West. Bonchō arrives from Kyōto; Kyorai returns to the capital. In the early evening I retire to bed.

20TH DAY

The nun Ukō[9] arrives to see the festival of North Saga. Kyorai comes up from Kyōto and recites a poem written on the way:

> squabbling children,
>   the same height as
>   the barley in the field
> *tsukamiau / kodomo no take ya / mugibatake* (Kyorai)

The Villa of Fallen Persimmons remains as it was when the previous owner built it, but here and there it is deteriorating. The melancholy of its condition draws my heart more than if it were new. The carved beams and wall paintings have been rav-

aged by winds and drenched with rains. Curious rocks and
strangely shaped trees are hidden under overgrown vines. In
front of the bamboo verandah is a single citron tree,[10] with aro-
matic blossoms.

> citron blossoms—
>   let's recall the olden days:
>   the food preparing room.
> *yu no hana ya / mukashi shinobamu / ryōri no ma*

> cuckoo:
>   filtering through the vast bamboo grove
>   the moon's light
> *hototogisu / ōtakeyabu o / moru tsukiyo*

The Nun Ukō:

> I'll come again:
>   ripen once more, strawberries
>   of Saga mountain
> *mata ya kon / ichigo akarame / saga no yama* (Ukō)

The wife of Kyorai's elder brother has sent us sweets and
side dishes of food. Tonight, Ukō and Bonchō stay with us,
making five people[11] under a single mosquito net. Sleep is difficult and past midnight each of us gets up, so we bring out the
sweets and wine cups from the afternoon and talk till dawn.
Last summer, when Bonchō slept at my house, four of us from
four provinces[12] slept under a two-mat mosquito net. "Four
thoughts, and so four different types of dreams," someone said
in jest, and we all laughed. Morning comes, Ukō and Bonchō
return to Kyōto, while Kyorai stays on.

21ST DAY

Having slept but little last night, I don't feel well today. Even the
sky has changed: cloudy since dawn, with the sound of rain now
and then. Most of the day I just lie around, nodding off. As
night approaches, Kyorai returns to Kyōto. I'm all alone in the

evening, but since I slept during the day, I cannot fall asleep tonight. I take out notes jotted down at the Unreal Dwelling and make finished drafts.

22ND DAY

Rain through the morning. No visitors, and in my loneliness I amuse myself with random writing, including the following: He who mourns makes sorrow his master; he who drinks makes pleasure his master. When Saigyō wrote,[13] "were there no loneliness, I would be in misery," he made loneliness his master. In another poem he wrote:

> In this mountain hamlet
>   whom are you calling to
>   little cuckoo?
> I had come here thinking
>   I would live all alone.[255]
> *yamazato ni / ko wa mata tare o / yobukodori /*
> *hitori sumamu to / omoishi mono o*

Nothing is as alluring as solitude. The recluse Chōshō[15] wrote: "if a guest gains a half a day of quiet leisure, the host loses a half day of quiet leisure." Sodō often meditated admiringly on those words. And so I too,

> sunk in sorrow,
>   make me feel loneliness:
>   mountain cuckoo
> *uki ware o / sabishigarase yo / kankodori*

I wrote this verse while staying alone at a certain temple.[16]

In the evening I receive a letter from Kyorai. It says that Otokuni[17] has returned from Edo with many letters from old friends and disciples. Among them Kyokusui reports that he visited the old site of the Bashō Hut I used to live in and met Sōha[18] there.

long ago
   who cleaned the small pots?
     violet blossoms
mukashi tare / konabe araishi / sumiregusa (Sōha)

He also writes: "Where I now live there is nothing green
save for a single maple the length of two bows."[19]

young maple:
   leaves the rich brown
     of a single flourishing
waka kaede / chairo ni naru mo / hito sakari (Sōha)

In Ransetsu's letter

collected among
   the dust of the osmund ferns:
     brackens[20]
zenmai no / chiri ni eraruru / warabi kana (Ransetsu)

servant changing day—
   in the hearts of the children,
     the sadness of things
degawari ya / osanagokoro ni / mono aware
(Ransetsu)

In the other letters are many things deeply moving that
bring such longing.

23RD DAY

clapping hands,
   and dawnlight in the echo:
     summer moon
te o uteba / kodama ni akuru / natsu no tsuki

bamboo shoots—
   and my childhood
     sketches of them
take no ko ya / osanaki toki no / e no susami

day by day
the barley reddens toward ripeness:
singing skylarks
hitohi hitohi / mugi akaramite / naku hibari

devoid of talent,
I wish only to sleep:
raucous warblers
nō nashi no / nemutashi ware o / gyōgyōshi

Topic: Villa of Fallen Persimmons

the beanfield
and firewood shed too:
celebrated sites
mame uuru / hata mo kibeya mo / meisho kana
(Bonchō)

As nightfall approached, Kyorai comes up from Kyōto. A letter from Shōbō[21] of Zeze. And one from Shōhaku of Ōtsu. Bonchō arrives. The Abbot[263] of Honpuku Temple in Katada drops by and spends the night. Bonchō returns to Kyōto.

25TH DAY

Senna returns to Ōtsu. Fumikuni and Jōsō stop by to visit.

Topic: Villa of Fallen Persimmons. By Jōsō.

Deep in Saga facing the mountains, with birds and
fish as companions,
Dwelling joyfully in the wilderness, as if in the
abode of a recluse.
The tips of the branches still lack the eggs of the red
dragon,[23]
But the green leaves are thick with poetic themes,
conducive to writing.

Seeking Lady Kogō's Grave. By Jōsō:

> Anguished by strong resentments, she fled the impe-
> rial palace,
> The round moon of autumn above her, the wind
> through the country village.
> In those distant years, the minister found her by the
> sound of her koto.
> Where now is her lonesome grave among these
> bamboo groves?

> budding forth
>   into a flourish of sprouts:
>   persimmon seeds
> *medashi yori / futaba ni shigeru / kaki no sane*
> (Fumikuni)

A song along the road

> a cuckoo
>   sings—the hackberry
>   like the plum and cherry[24]
> *hototogisu / naku ya enoki mo / ume sakura* (Jōsō)

An inspiring poem by Huang Tingjian[25]

> Chen Wuji was absorbed in poetry, leaving his
> guests at the gate;
> Qin Shaoyu welcomed his guests, and then resumed
> wielding his brush.

Otokuni arrives and speaks of Edo. Also brings a one-inch
candle renku,[26] which includes the following links:[27]

> a lay monk's
>   medicine box
>   close to his breast[28]
> *hanzoku no / kōyakuire wa / futokori ni*

> Usui mountain pass:
>   it's wise to go by horse
> *usui no tōge / uma zo kashikoki* (Kikaku)

* * *

fish basket at his hip,
   brimming with moon madness
   koshi no ajika ni / kuruwasuru tsuki

after an autumn windstorm
   handing it over to an exile:
      a small shack[29]
nowaki yori / runin ni watasu / koya hitotsu (Kikaku)

* * *

at Mount Utsu
   borrowing from a woman
      nightwear to sleep in
utsu no yama / onna ni yo yogi o / karite neru

accused of a lie,
   she is pardoned on Purification Day[30]
itsuwari semete / yurusu shōjin (Kikaku)

    After the hour of the monkey,[31] wind, rain, and violent thunder, and hail falls. The size of the hail is about three *momme*,[32] the large ones the size of apricots, the small ones that of *shiba* chestnuts. When the dragon[33] passes out of the sky, the hail begins.

26TH DAY

budding forth
   into a flourish of sprouts:
      persimmon seeds
medashi yori / futaba ni shigeru / kaki no sane
(Fumikuni)

like dust over the field,
   scattering deutzia blossoms[34]
hatake no chiri ni / kakaru unohana (Bashō)

a snail,
    unsure of itself,
        waves its horns
katatsumuri / tanomoshigenaki / tsuno furite (Kyorai)

while someone draws the well-water
    I wait for the bucket
hito no kumu ma o / tsurube matsu nari (Jōsō)

the dawn moon:
    is it the weekly courier
        coming down the road?[35]
ariake ni / sando bikyaku no / yuku yaran (Otokuni)

27TH DAY

No visitors. I have quiet leisure all day long.

28TH DAY

In a dream I begin to speak of Tokoku, then awake weeping. Whenever spirits commune, dreams come. When *yin* is exhausted, there are dreams of fire; when *yang* withers away, one dreams of water. If a bird in flight carries hair in its beak, one dreams of flying; if you sleep on your sash, you dream of snakes. The famous dreams of Shui-zhen Ji, Huai-an Guo, and Zhuang Zhou accorded with principle; there is nothing strange about them.

My dreams certainly aren't those of sages or true gentlemen. All day my spirit is scattered with delusions; at night my dreams are the same. Dreaming about Tokoku is called a "remembering" dream. He was deeply devoted to me, and came seeking me all the way to my home village of Iga. We shared the same bed at night, we comforted each other from the aches of our journeys, and for a hundred days he was my companion, steadfast as a shadow. At times we frolicked together; at times we grieved. His deep feeling penetrated to the bottom of my

heart; I will never forget him. Waking from my dream, my
sleeves are drenched with tears.

29TH DAY

I look over poems on Takadachi in Ōshū from *Single Poems by
Individual Poets.*

LAST DAY OF THE MONTH

"Takadachi soars into the heavens like a star on a helmet. The
Koromo river flows into the sea and the moon is like a bow."
Such a portrayal of the landscape is not true to the scene. Unless
one actually travels to the place,[36] even the great ancients can't
make authentic poems.

1ST DAY OF THE MONTH

Riyū of Meishō Temple in Hirata in Gōshū calls on me.[37] Letters
from Shōhaku and Senna arrive.

> bamboo sprouts—
>   the ones left unused
>   now covered with dew
> *take no ko ya / kuinokosareshi / ato no tsuyu* (Riyū)

> for these days
>   summer underwear's just right:
>   Fifth Month
> *kono goro no / hadagi mi ni tsuku / uzuki kana*
> (Shōhaku)

> long-awaited,
>   the Fifth Month draws near:
>   bridegroom's rice-cake[38]
> *mataretsuru / satsuki mo chikashi / mukochimaki*
> (Shōhaku)

2ND DAY

Sora arrives and tells me about seeing the blossoms of Yoshino
and his pilgrimage to Kumano. He speaks of my old friends and
disciples in Edo and we talk about this and that.

the trail into Kumano—
    making our way through and:
        summer's sea
kumanoji ya / waketsutsuireba / natsu no umi (Sora)

Mount Ōmine—
    deep into Yoshino,
        the last blooms
ōmine ya / yoshino no oku o / hana no hate (Sora)

As the sun begins to set, we head off by boat on the Ōi River
along Mount Arashi up to Tonase. Rain begins to fall, and as
night comes on, we return home.

3RD DAY

Last night's rain fell on and on, then all through today and
tonight. We talk of Edo, and night turns to day.

4TH DAY

Having stayed up all night, I'm exhausted and sleep all day.
Around noon the rain stops. Tomorrow I leave the Villa of
Fallen Persimmons, a departure I deeply regret. The inner room,
the entryway . . . I wander through each room, a last look.

early summer rains—
    poem cards peeled off,
        traces on the wall
samidare ya / shikishi hegitaru / kabe no ato

Selected *Haibun*

Brushwood Gate 94
Live Austere and Clear 94
Sleeping Alone in a Grass Hut 94
Old Beggar 95
Words on a Cold Night 96
Written on a Painting of "Summer Fields" 96
Introduction to "Empty Chestnuts" 97
Praise for a Linked Verse 97
On Mount Fuji 98
Asleep on Horseback 98
The Sound of Hulling Rice 98
Deep in Bamboo 99
Preface to "beat the fulling block" 99
Preface to "wild poem: in winter's winds" 100
Single Branch Eaves 101
Introduction to the Picture Scroll of
    "Journal of Bleached Bones in a Field" 101
Three Names 102
Plums by the Hedge 102
Introduction to "Ise Travel Journal" 103
First Snow 104
Great Ball of Snow 104

ADMONITION ABOUT THE RECLUSIVE LIFE 104
A PLUM IN A GROVE 105
POSTSCRIPT TO "COMMENTS ON THE BAGWORM" 105
THE VILLAGE OF HOBI 106
VISITING ISE SHRINE 107
PREFACE TO "ALL THE MORE I WANT TO SEE IT" 107
FALSE CYPRESS 107
FOREWORD TO "CLIMBING MOUNT KŌYA" 108
PREFACE TO "VILLAGERS" 108
AN ACCOUNT OF EIGHTEEN VIEW TOWER 109
CORMORANT FISHING BOAT 110
AN ACCOUNT OF THE MOON AT OBASUTE
    IN SARASHINA 110
10TH DAY CHRYSANTHEMUMS AT SODŌ'S HOUSE 111
A STAFF OF WITHERED WOOD 111
SENT TO ETSUJIN 112
PREFACE TO THE "WIDE FIELDS" LINKED-VERSE
    COLLECTION 112
PREFACE TO "A GRASS HUT TOO" 113
PREFACE TO "A MAN CARRYING FODDER" 113
CONCERNING THE BEAUTIFUL SCENERY AT THE
    HOME OF MASTER SHŪA 113
SUMMER'S CUCKOO 114
PREFACE TO "ACROSS THE PLAIN" 114
CUCKOO AT A LODGING IN TAKAKU 115
OKU'S RICE-PLANTING SONG 115
PREFACE TO "A HIDDEN HOUSE" 116
PATTERN RUBBING ROCK 116
PREFACE TO "RAIN HAT ISLAND" 117
MATSUSHIMA 117
MEMORIAL FOR HIGH PRIEST TENYŪ 118
PREFACE TO SILVER RIVER 119

IN PRAISE OF A HOT SPRING 119
IN TSURUGA 120
AKECHI'S WIFE 121
AN ACCOUNT OF PURE WASHED HALL 122
WORDS FOR THE BROKEN PESTLE MALLET 122
AN ACCOUNT OF THE UNREAL DWELLING 123
PROSE POEM ON THE UNREAL DWELLING 126
EVENING COOL AT RIVERSIDE, FOURTH AVENUE 128
ON A PORTRAIT BY UNCHIKU 128
ON A PORTRAIT OF SOTOBA KOMACHI 129
RECORD OF A VILLA OF FALLEN PERSIMMONS 129
ON THE NIGHT OF THE 16TH AT KATADA BAY 130
WORDS IN PRAISE OF THE PINE OF
    NARIHIDE'S GARDEN 131
AMIDABŌ 132
STAYING OVER AT RIYŪ'S PLACE AT MENSHŌ TEMPLE . . . 132
EARLY WINTER SHOWER AT SHIMADA 133
WITHERED MISCANTHUS IN SNOW 133
WORDS ON LEAVING THE NEST 134
WORDS ON TRANSPLANTING THE *BASHŌ* TREE (1) . . . 134
WORDS ON TRANSPLANTING THE *BASHŌ* TREE (2) . . . 135
FAREWELL TO TŌZAN 136
IN PRAISE OF A DESK 137
PRAISE FOR A PAINTING OF THREE SAGES 137
WORDS OF FAREWELL TO KYORIKU 138
WORDS SENT TO KYORIKU 139
AN EXPLANATION OF SECLUSION 140
LIFE OF TŌJUN 141
VISITING SODŌ'S CHRYSANTHEMUM GARDEN 141
PREFACE TO "LIGHTNING" 142
CONSTRUCTING A HAT 142

BRUSHWOOD GATE

After nine springs and autumns of a lonely, austere life in the city, I have moved to the bank of the Fukagawa River. Someone[1] once said, "Since of old, Chang-an has been a place for fame and fortune—and so hard for a wayfarer empty-handed and penniless." Is it because I'm impoverished myself that I can understand his feelings?

> against the brushwood gate
>   it sweeps the tea leaves:
>   storm wind
> *shiba no to ni / cha o konoha kaku / arashi kana*

Autumn, 1680

* * *

LIVE AUSTERE AND CLEAR

Lonely poverty, gazing at the moon. Lonely poverty, contemplating my low state. Lonely poverty, thinking about my lack of talent. How am I doing? Let me answer, "in lonely poverty"... but no one responds. More lonely poverty.[2]

> live austere and clear!
>   the recluse moongazer's
>   tea drinking song
> *wabite sume / tsukiwabisai ga / naracha uta*

Autumn, 1681

* * *

SLEEPING ALONE IN A GRASS HUT

The Elder Du[3] wrote a poem of a thatched hut tearing in the wind.[4] Then old man Su Shi, moved by the lonely poverty[5] in that poem, wrote a verse about a leaking cottage. Now I listen to their rain on the banana leaves, lying alone in my grass hut.

banana plant in a windstorm:
a night of listening
to rain in a tub
bashō nowaki shite / tarai ni ame o / kiku yo kana

Autumn, 1681

* * *

OLD BEGGAR

In my window, snow of a thousand autumns on a western
peak.
By my gate, ships waiting to sail a thousand leagues across the
eastern sea.[6]
—Master of the Hall of Ships at Anchor, Flower Tōsei[7]

I can make out the poem but can't enter into the feelings. I rec-
ognize the lonely poverty, but don't fathom its deep delight. I
surpass the Elder Du only in the frequency of my illnesses.
Hidden in the banana leaves by my meager hut, I call myself
"Old Man Beggar."

the oars' sound striking the waves,
my bowels freezing,
night—and tears
rosei nami o utte / harawata kōru / yo ya namida

at a poor mountain temple,
a kettle crying in the frost,
the voice frigid
hinzan no / kama shimo ni naku / koe samushi

Buying water at this thatched hut

ice is bitter
in the mouth of the rat
quenching its thirst
kōri nigaku / enso ga nodo o / uruoseri

the year ending
    with echoes of pounding rice-cakes—
      a desolate sleep
kurekurete / mochi o kodama no / wabine kana

                                        Autumn, 1681

                    * * *

WORDS ON A COLD NIGHT

By the fork of the river in Fukagawa, I live lonely and poor in a
grass-thatched hut. I gaze on the snow peak of Mount Fuji in
the distance and at ships of a thousand leagues nearby. At dawn,
the white wake of a boat heading off.[8] Through the evening, the
dream of wind through withered reeds.[9] Sitting in the moon's
light, I lament my empty cask; lying in bed, I grieve over my thin
quilt.

    the oars' sound striking the waves,
        my bowels freezing,
          night—and tears
ro no koe nami o utte / harawata kōru / yo ya namida

                                        Winter, 1681–82

                    * * *

WRITTEN ON A PAINTING OF "SUMMER FIELDS"

"That monk who's wearing a hat and riding a horse, where's he
coming from, what's he after?" "That," replied the painter, "is a
portrait of you on a journey." "Well, if so, bumbling wayfarer of
the three worlds,[10] watch out you don't topple from that horse."

    the horse ambling,
        I see myself in a painting:
          summer fields
uma bokuboku / ware o e ni miru / natsuno kana

                                        Summer, 1683

                    * * *

INTRODUCTION TO "EMPTY CHESTNUTS"[11]

This one book called "chestnuts" has four tastes. The first is like drinking the wine of the poetic heart of Li Bo and Du Fu.[12] Another is like eating the rice gruel of Han Shan's[13] dharma. These poems have the subtlety of something seen far away or heard from a great distance.[14] Then there is the rare flavor of lonely poverty and elegance:[15] it is found at the mountain home of Saigyō in the wormy chestnuts that people ignore.[16]

The fourth taste plumbs the feelings of love in various circumstances. The image of Xi Shi's face hidden in her hanging sleeves has been carved like gold into the figure of Komurasaki.[17] In the neglected bedrooms of the ladies of Xuan Zong's court, ivy hung down from the clothes racks. In the lower classes there are women who are raised hidden in the recesses of their houses, ever-accompanied by their parents, while brides feud with their mothers-in-law. The stories of love from temple boys and young Kabuki actors are not neglected. In such matters, Bo Juyi serves as a guide to haikai novices as his poetry is turned into Japanese verse.

The expression of these poems is ever shifting, and one cannot distinguish between truth and falsehood. These verse are forged like the Yellow Emperor's tripod[18] and the words are smelted in the dragon spring. This treasure is the work of no one other than Kikaku, and the thieves of poetry lie in wait.

Third year of Tenna, frolicing in mid-summer.

Summer, 1683

* * *

PRAISE FOR A LINKED VERSE

A windstorm from Pine Mountain[19] in the province of Iyo has blown upon the withered leaves at Bashō Cave, and its voice sings a linked verse. Ah, the distant sound of wind, the rustling of leaves: like the ringing of a jewel, the echoes of gold and iron—sometimes blowing forcefully, sometimes soft. They arouse such deep feelings,[20] bringing forth tears. Through a thousand holes comes a fierce roar, the echoes ever shifting, the meanings of each verse distinct. This is heaven's spontaneous piping,[21] a wafting wind that tears the banana leaves.

1683?

* * *

ON MOUNT FUJI

Mount Kunlun[22] is said to be far away, and in Mount Penglai and Mount Fangzhang[23] dwell Daoist immortals. But right here before my eyes: Mount Fuji's great peak rises from the earth. It seems to hold up the blue heavens and open the cloud gate for the sun and moon. From wherever I gaze, there is a consummate vista as the beautiful scenery goes through a thousand changes. Even poets can't exhaust this scene in verse; those with great talent and men of letters give up their words; painters too abandon their brushes and flee. If the demigods of faraway Gushe Mountain[24] were to appear, I wonder if even they could succeed in putting this scene into a poem or a painting.

> with clouds and mist
> in a brief moment a hundred scenes
> brought to fulfillment[25]
> *kumokiri no / zanji hyakkei o / tsukushikeri*

Autumn, 1684

* * *

ASLEEP ON HORSEBACK

The waning moon shown pale in the sky, and the base of the hills was still dark. I tottered on my horse, almost falling a number of times. Crossing many miles before any sound of cockcrow, I rode in a lingering dream as in Du Mu's[26] "Dawn Departure." As I arrived at Sayo-no-nakayama, I was startled awake.

dozing on my horse,
with dream lingering and moon distant:
smoke from a tea fire
uma ni nete / zanmu tsuki tōshi / cha no keburi

Autumn, 1684

* * *

THE SOUND OF HULLING RICE

The town called Nagao in the province of Yamato is not far
from the capital. It is a mountain village like no other. The
master of this house is a man of deep sensitivity and understanding. Next to the main house he has prepared a place for his
mother to live. In the garden he has cultivated fascinating plants
and set curious boulders. By his own hand, he has trained the
branches and arranged the rocks. "I want this mountain to
become Mount Penglai—so I can obtain the elixir of long life
for my mother," he said, showing his deep sincerity in taking
care for his mother. It is said that when a family is poor, filial
piety will be expressed. This man fulfills that virtue without
being poor, something even the ancients said is difficult.

a home that knows no winter—
the hulling of rice
sounds like hail
fuyu shiranu / yado wa momisuru / oto are

Ninth Month, 1684

* * *

DEEP IN BAMBOO

I stayed several days at a place called Takenouchi in Yamato.
The village headman came to visit me day and night to help
soothe the sorrows of my journey. He is truly no ordinary man.
His heart sports in the highest realms, while his body mixes with
grasscutters and woodsmen, with hunters of pheasants and

hares. Carrying a hoe, he makes his way to the fields of Tao Qian.[27] Leading an ox, he follows the hermit of Mount Ji.[28] In this way he throws himself into his work, never tiring. His house may seem lowly, but he delights in his poverty. One who can attain tranquillity even in the city—such is this man.

> the cotton-beating bow—
>   biwa sounds that bring solace
>   deep in the bamboo[29]
> *watayumi ya / biwa ni nagusamu / take no oku*

Ninth Month, 1684

* * *

PREFACE TO "BEAT THE FULLING BLOCK"

Alone I spent the night in the depths of Yoshino. The mountains were so deep. White clouds lay piled on the peaks, and misty rain filled the valley. The sound of wood cut to the west echoed on the east. Temple bells struck to the base of my heart. I took lodging at a temple.

> beat the fulling block,
>   make me hear it—
>   temple wife
> *kinuta uchite / ware ni kikaseyo ya / bō ga tsuma*

Autumn, 1684

* * *

PREFACE TO "WILD POEM: IN WINTER'S WINDS"

My hat has fallen apart in the rains of this long journey, and my paper coat is crumpled from night after night of storms. I'm so completely disheveled I can't help feeling compassion for my miserable state. Then it occurred to me that long ago a master of wild poetry had journeyed to this province.

a wild poem:
    in winter's winds
      don't I look
        just like Chikusai[30]
  kyōku / kogarashi no / mi wa chikusai ni / nitaru kana

Winter, 1684–85

* * *

SINGLE BRANCH EAVES

The good doctor Genzui has gathered great experience and is able to cure both household illness and epidemics. He has called his house "Single Branch Eaves." This must be because he feels that his accomplishments are not even a single flower of a branch in a great forest, that they don't even come close to the flowered branch that gave rise to Kasyapa's subtle smile.[31] The True Man of the Southern Flower, Zhuangzi, delighted in a nest on a single branch. The ditch rat fills his belly and plays in the country of Not-Even-Anything.[32] Genzui's desire is to awaken those with the firey evil of foolish delusions, to cure one-sided thinking and small-mindedness.

a wren of a single branch:
    the fragrance of its plum blossoms
      throughout the world
  yo ni nioi / baika isshi no / misosazai

Spring 1685

* * *

INTRODUCTION TO THE PICTURE SCROLL OF "JOURNAL OF BLEACHED BONES IN A FIELD"

This work does not quite fit the genre of travel journal. It's just a record of the movements of the heart through scenes of mountain bridges and country stores. Nakagawa Jokushi has applied his painting colors to a scroll of the journal, making up for my inability to depict the scenes in words. If others see his paintings, I'll certainly feel ashamed.

> spend nights on a journey,
>   then you'll know my poems—
>   autumn wind
> *tabine shite / waga ku o shire ya / aki no kaze*

Winter, 1685–86

* * *

THREE NAMES

All through the night the sky kept shifting between clear and cloudy, leaving us restless.

> clouds now and then
>   give us a rest:
>   moonviewing[33]
> *kumo oriori / hito o yasumuru / tsukimi kana*

Three men living in Reiganjima visited my grass-thatched hut as night deepened. When I asked their names, it turned out that they shared the same name, Shichirobei. Recalling Li Bo's poem about drinking alone, I playfully wrote:

> with a full wine cup
>   I drink to three names
>   this evening[34]
> *sakazuki ni / mitsu no na o nomu / koyoi kana*

15th of Eighth Month, 1685

* * *

PLUMS BY THE HEDGE

I went to see a certain person at his hermitage, but an old man caretaking the hut said, "the master is off on a temple pilgrimage." The plums by the hedge were in full bloom so I replied,

"These will take his place—they look like him." To which he responded, "Well, actually, they belong to the neighbors."

> arriving when you were out,
>   even the plums are far away
>   beyond the hedge
> *rusu ni kite / ume sae yoso no / kakio kana*

Spring, 1686?

* * *

INTRODUCTION TO "ISE TRAVEL JOURNAL"

Like a rootless plant without flower or fruit, haikai today is merely vulgar banter and sporting with words. But one year Kikaku, during a journey's rest under the sky of the capital, became close to Mukai Kyorai. They drank sake and over tea they talked of the waters of the heart—the sweet, the bitter, the astringent, the pale. Kikaku related its character from the shallows to the depths until the taste of a hundred rivers could be realized in one drink.

During autumn of this year Kyorai made a pilgrimage to Ise with his younger sister. As the autumn wind of Shirakawa blew, he slept by the reeds of Ise and wrote of the deep feelings of the places where he stayed. Now he has sent off his words to the desk of this hut. When I read it the first time my feelings were aroused. Rereading it, I was entranced, my feelings forgotten. Reading it a third time I realized the work's perfect tranquillity. This Kyorai has fully arrived at the Way.

> east and west
>   the deep feeling is but one:
>   autumn wind
> *higashi nishi / awaresa hitotsu / aki no kaze*

Autumn, 1686

* * *

FIRST SNOW

I hoped to view the first snow at my grass hut, so whenever if I happened to be somewhere else, as soon as the sky would cloud over, I rushed home—many times I did this. Then on the 8th of Twelfth Month, I was overjoyed as snow fell for the first time.

first snow—
      great luck to be here
         in my own hut
hatsu yuki ya / saiwai an ni / makariaru

Winter, 1686–87

* * *

A GREAT BALL OF SNOW

A man named Sora has set up temporary lodging nearby, and morning and night we visit each other. When I cook something, he helps by feeding the fire; when I make tea, he breaks up ice for water. By nature he loves quiet solitude, and our friendship is greater than gold. One evening he visited in a snowfall.

you start a fire,
      I'll show you something fun:
         a great ball of snow
kimi hi o take / yoki mono misen / yuki maruge

Winter, 1686–87

* * *

ADMONITION ABOUT THE RECLUSIVE LIFE

Ah, lazy old man. Usually visitors are so wearisome, and I vow deep in my heart, "I won't meet them; no, I won't invite them," but then the night's moon comes or the morning snow, and I yearn for friends—I just can't help it. I sit in silence, drinking sake all alone, spinning questions in my mind. I push open the door of my hut, I gaze out upon the snow, once again picking up my wine cup, dipping my brush and dropping it down. Ah, mad old man.

> drinking sake
> and now it's harder to sleep:
> night of snow
> *sake nomeba / itodo nerarene / yoru no yuki*

Winter, 1686–87?

* * *

A PLUM IN A GROVE

Last year while journeying to the capital, I met a pilgrim monk on the road. This spring, off to see the deep north of Oku, he stopped by for a visit.

> come visit again:
> in the grove,
> a plum blossom
> *mata mo toe / yabu no naka naru / ume no hana*

Spring, 1687

* * *

POSTSCRIPT TO "COMMENTS ON THE BAGWORM"

I shut myself inside this grass hut, and while living in lonely poverty, I happened to come up with a poem about a bagworm. My friend Yamaguchi Sodō was deeply moved by it and wrote a Chinese poem and essay. In the poem he has embroidered brocade, and the essay is like a rolled jewel. When I savor it, it seems to have the skill of Ju Yuan's "Encountering Sorrow," the freshness of Su Shi, and the novelty of Huang Shangu.

In the beginning, he speaks of the filial piety of Emperor Shun and Ceng Can, giving them as examples for people to follow. Admiring those lacking talent and craft, he says we should look again to the heart of Zhuangzi. In the end, he cites the bagworm's licentious relationship with a jewel bug, admonishing against lust. Were it not for venerable Sodō, who would understand the heart of the bagworm? Someone once said, "if one looks with tranquillity, one sees that all things are self-realized." Thanks to this person, one can understand my poem. From long ago, people who took up the brush have embellished the flower of writing's beauty while the fruit of its meaning grew weak. Or they dwelled on the fruit and forgot the art. But with Sodō's writing, we can love the flower and also feast on the fruit.

There is a painter named Chōko who, when he heard of the bagworm poem, created a painting for it. Truly the colors are pale but the feeling is deep. If we turn our heart to it, the worm seems to move and one wonders if the gold leaves are falling. If we bend our ears and listen closely, the worm seems to call out as the autumn wind murmurs and brings a chill.

Now in a quiet moment by a window, I receive the blessing of these two men—such is the great honor of the bagworm.[35]

Autumn, 1687

* * *

THE VILLAGE OF HOBI

According to the people here, this village is called "Hobi" because in olden times a retired emperor praised it, saying "preserve its beauty" (*ho bi*). I don't know where this might be written down, but such gracious sentiment is awe-inspiring.

> plum and camellia:
>   praise to their early bloom
>   here in Hobi Village
> *ume tsubaki / hayazaki homen / hobi no sato*

Cape Irago was close by, so I went to see it.

> Cape Irago:
>   nothing can match
>   the hawk's cry
> *iragozaki / niru mono mo nashi / taka no koe*

Eleventh Month, 1687

* * *

VISITING THE ISE SHRINE

Near the end of Second Month, fifth year of Jōkyō, I traveled to Ise, the fifth time I set foot on the hollowed ground in front of the shrine. I had aged yet another year, so I felt more keenly the divine light and august majesty of the place. With deep yearning I recalled that Saigyō in tears wrote of feeling blessed here.[36] Spreading my fan on the sand, I bowed my head onto it.

> from what tree's
>   blossoms I know not:
>   such fragrance
> *nani no ki no / hana to wa shirazu / nioi kana*

Second Month, 1688

* * *

PREFACE TO "ALL THE MORE I WANT TO SEE IT"

I was on pilgrimage in Yamato Province crossing over the foothills of Mount Kazuraki. The cherry blossoms in all four directions in full bloom, and with haze spreading across peak after peak, the appearance of dawn was exquisitely beautiful. It is said that the god here, Hitokotonushi-no-kami, has a hideous face, and people of the world have reviled him, so I wrote:

> all the more I want to see it
>   with dawn coming to the blossoms:
>   the face of the god
> *nao mitashi / hana ni akeyuku / kami no kao*

Spring, 1688

* * *

FALSE CYPRESS

"Tomorrow I will become a cypress!" an old tree in a valley once said. Yesterday has passed as a dream; tomorrow has not yet come. Instead of just enjoying a cask of wine in my life,[37] I keep saying "tomorrow, tomorrow," securing the reproof of the sages.

> loneliness—
>   among the blossoms
>   a false cypress[38]
> *sabishisa ya / hana no atari no / asunarō*

Spring, 1688

* * *

PREFACE TO "CLIMBING MOUNT KŌYA"

I climbed into the depths of Kōya[39] where the lamp of the Law is never extinguished. The area is filled with the lodgings of monks and believers, with the tile roofs of the great temples lined up close together. With spring's blossoms, which open like the sudden enlightenment upon a mudra, I sense the fragrant glow of a sky misty with the peace of realization. With the call of the monkeys and cries of birds, my heart is wrenched. I pray with a quiet heart at Kūkai's mausoleum and then linger around the ossuary, deep in thought. Here the remains of so many are collected, from the hair of my ancestors down to the white bones of all those whom I am close to and those who are so dear. As I make offerings deep in sorrow, my sleeves cannot stop my flowing tears. At last I hold them back and write:

> for my father and mother
>   I yearn so deeply—
>   a pheasant's cry[40]
> *chichi haha no / shikiri ni kanashi / kiji no koe*

Spring, 1688

* * *

PREFACE TO "VILLAGERS"

The lotus is called the Lord of Flowers. The peony is said to be the wealthy nobility among blossoms. But rice seedlings rise from the mud, and are more pure than the lotus. In autumn, it yields fragrant rice, richer than the peony. Thus, one plant combines the virtues of both, truly pure and rich.

> villagers sing
>   verses in the rice fields:
>   the capital
> *satobito wa / ine ni uta yomu / miyako kana*

Fourth Month, 1688

* * *

AN ACCOUNT OF EIGHTEEN VIEW TOWER

In Mino there is a stately mansion facing the Nagara River whose owner is named Kashima. Behind it tower the Inaba Mountains and to the west a disturbance of mountains cluster together, neither close by nor far away. A temple in the rice fields is hidden by a stand of cryptomeria and bamboo surrounding the homes along the river bank is deep green. Here and there bleached cloth is stretched out to dry, and to the right a ferry boat floats by. The townsfolk busily go back and forth, the eaves of this fishing village are lined up close together, and fishermen are pulling in the nets and dangling fishing lines. All this seems to enhance for the viewer the enjoyment of the scene.

Enchanted, I forget the summer day, which seems to hold off the coming dark. The light of the setting sun changes into the moon; the light of the fishing fires, too, formed on the waves, slowly approaches. The cormorant fishing under the high railing is a truly striking spectacle. The eight views of the Xiao River and the ten sites of the Xiang River are experienced together in the one flavor of the cool wind. If I were to give a name to this mansion, I might call it the Eighteen View Manor.

> in this area
>   all that meets the eye
>   is cool
> *kono atari / me ni miyuru mono wa / mina suzushi*

Fifth year of Jōkyō, mid-summer.

Mid-summer, 1688

* * *

CORMORANT FISHING BOAT

The cormorant fishing of Nagara River at Shō in Gifu is famous throughout the country and it is as fascinating as the accounts. Without wisdom and talent, I cannot possibly exhaust the scene in words, but I long to show it to those whose heart understands. Saying these things I returned to an inn on the dark road of Yamiji. As it says in the Nō play "Cormorant Fishing," "How regrettable the parting from Yamaji."

> fascinating,
>   and then sorrowful:
>   cormorant boat
> *omoshirōte / yagate kanashiki / ubune kana*

Sixth Month, 1688

* * *

AN ACCOUNT OF THE MOON AT
MOUNT OBASUTE IN SARASHINA

I have often been enticed on hearing of Shirara and Fukiage, and this year an intense yearning arose to see the moon at Obasute. Heading off from Mino Province on the eleventh day of Eighth Month—the journey long and the days few[41]—I departed as evening came on, seeking a grass pillow when darkness fell. As I had hoped, I made it to Sarashina Village for the night of the harvest moon. The mountain runs southwesterly, about one league south of the village of Yawata. It is not particularly high, the rocks are not rugged, yet the whole mountain is permeated with the deep sadness of things. It is said that here "it is so difficult to be consoled"[42] and now I see why. I couldn't help grieving as I wondered how people could have abandoned elderly women, and the tears that fell compounded my melancholy.

> her face—
>   an old woman weeping alone:
>   moon as companion
> *omokage wa / oba hitori naku / tsuki no tomo*

moon of the sixteenth
and still I linger here
near Sarashina
izayoi mo / mada sarashina no / kōri kana

Eighth Month, 1688

* * *

10TH DAY CHRYSANTHEMUMS AT SODŌ'S HOUSE

Fifth year of Jōkyō, middle of the month of Chrysanthemum
and the Moon.
The old master of this lotus pond loves chrysanthemums.
Yesterday, there was a celebration at Mount Lu,[43] and today we
drink the rest of the wine, each of us sporting with making
verse. We wonder now, who among us will enjoy good health
next year on this day?

10th day chrysanthemums[44]

the sixteenth night moon?
or is it this morning's lingering
chrysanthemums?
izayoi no / izure ka kesa ni / nokoru kiku

Ninth Month, 1688

* * *

A STAFF OF WITHERED WOOD[45]

I had heard the good name of the Buddhist layman Dōen of
Daitsūan Hut. With warm feelings toward him, I promised that
we would meet, but before that day could come, he passed away
like the frost of an early winter evening. Hearing that today is
the first anniversary of his death,

I long to imagine
how you looked—your staff
of withered wood
sono katachi / mibaya kareki no / tsue no take

Winter, 1688–89

* * *

SENT TO ETSUJIN

Jūzō of the province of Owari is known as Etsujin, a name that comes from the place where he was born. Now he hides himself in the city, but only to supply himself with some food and fuel. If he works two days, he plays the next two; if he works three days, he plays the next three. He loves his wine, and he sings from the *Tales of the Heike*[46] when he's drunk. A true friend indeed.

> that snow we saw:
>   this year also
>   has it fallen?[47]
> *futari mishi / yuki wa kotoshi mo / furikeru ka*

Winter, 1688–89

* * *

PREFACE TO THE "WIDE FIELDS" LINKED VERSE COLLECTION

Kakei is the master of Kyōbokudō in Nagoya, south of Owari, west of Atsuta. He edited a haikai collection and named it *Wide Fields*. Why he gave it that name I do not know, but from afar I offer the following conjecture. One year I was staying over at Nagoya and at various times we threw together some linked verse. He collected them and called it *Winter Sun*, and then extended the light with *Spring Sun*. They shone brilliantly in the world, like the sky of the Second and Third Months. They are like the willow and cherry rivaling brocade, like the distinct elegance of a butterfly or small bird, but perhaps the fruit is harmed a bit by such flowers. In this collection, a depth of heart emerges so faintly one can't be sure if it exists, like rising heat waves. On this path through a boundless landscape—like a red star lily clinging to nothing, a skylark free in the wide sky— Kakei will be our guide, watching over the vast field.

1689

* * *

PREFACE TO "A GRASS HUT TOO"

With the distant skies of the journey weighing on my mind, feeling apprehensive, I handed over the hut I had been living in to someone I knew. He was married with a daughter and baby.

> a grass hut too
>   has a season of moving:
>   a doll's house[48]
> *kusa no to mo / sumikawaru yo zo / hina no ie*

Third Month, 1689

* * *

PREFACE TO "A MAN CARRYING FODDER"

Thinking I would get to Michinoku, I set off for Shimozuke in hopes of finding the home of a certain Suitō in a town called Kurobane in Nasu Province. I had to push my way through the thick fields, the grass so deep I lost my way.

> a man carrying fodder:
>   I'll make him our guide
>   across this summer field
> *magusa ou / hito o shiori no / natsuno kana*

Fourth Month, 1689

* * *

CONCERNING THE BEAUTIFUL SCENERY AT THE HOME OF MASTER SHŪA

> mountains too
>   move into the garden—
>   a summer parlor
> *yama mo niwa ni / ugokiiruru ya / natsuzashiki*

A certain official at the Pure Dharma Temple is in charge of the Kurobane Manor in Nasu. His own residence too has nothing lowly about it and suits him well. The land extends to the summit, the mansion standing southeast. Curious peaks and a disturbance of ridges contend with each other, in hair-like strands of pale green as if in a painting. The sound of water, the call of birds, the green of pine and cryptomeria too in find detail and deep color: scenic beauty of consummate skill. The great accomplishments of the Creative—bringing such joy.

Summer, 1689

* * *

SUMMER'S CUCKOO

Whenever I wonder where the Shirakawa Barrier is, Priest Nōin's poem about the autumn wind comes to mind. Here I see only the green of barley sprouts and the poor farmers toiling painstakingly. Shirakawa is known for the deeply moving quality of spring and autumn and for viewing the moon and snow. But as Fourth Month gradually begins, I see not one of the hundred poetic scenes. I fall silent, abandoning my brush.

> rice fields and barley—
> and among them also
> summer's cuckoo
> *ta ya mugi ya / naka ni mo natsu no / hototogisu*

Fourth Month, 1689—

* * *

PREFACE TO "ACROSS THE PLAIN"

Traveling far across the Nasu Plain, we met someone who knew the area well.[49] He sent us off on horseback, a groom holding the reins. I wondered what was on his mind when he said, "Could you please write me a poem?" I thought, "What a remarkable and pleasant request, truly unusual," and I moistened the brush in my inkset and wrote on horseback,

across the plain,
turn my horse over there!
cuckoo

no o yoko ni / uma hikimuke yo / hototogisu

Fourth Month, 1689

* * *

CUCKOO AT A LODGING IN TAKAKU

As two monks on a pilgrimage to see Michinoku,[50] we visited
Shinohara in Nasu, and then thought of hurrying to see the
"Killing Rock" of Sesshōseki. But rain kept pouring down, so
we decided to stop over here first.

falling from high above—
at a Takaku lodging,
a cuckoo[51]

ochikuru ya / takaku no shuku no / hototogisu
(Gauze in the Wind)[52]

peering up through the branches
in the short night's rain[53]

ko no ma o nozoku / mijikayo no ame (Sora)

Second year of Genroku, early summer.

Fourth Month, 1689

* * *

OKU'S RICE-PLANTING SONG

My mind has been filled with thoughts of seeing the famous
places of the Deep North, and the remains of the old Shirakawa
Barrier especially drew my heart. I walked along the ancient
road, then crossed the present barrier. Finally I arrived in the
Iwase region[54] and knocked at the gate of Mr. Sagara Tōkyū.[55]
Then I departed this *yin* barrier[56] and meet some old friends.

the beginning of all art—
in the deep north
a rice-planting song[57]
fūryū no / hajime ya oku no / taueuta

Fourth Month, 1689

* * *

PREFACE TO "A HIDDEN HOUSE"

The monk Kashin has built a hut under a chestnut tree. It is said that long ago the Bodhisattva Gyōgi used the tree for his staff and the pillar of his hut because of its affinity with the Western Paradise. This hut has the spirit of seclusion and it calls to mind Amida's vows of universal salvation.

a hidden house—
the inconspicuous blossom
of a chestnut by the eaves
kakurega ya / medatanu hana o / noki no kuri

Fourth Month, 1689

* * *

PATTERN RUBBING ROCK

In the village called Shinobu,[58] in the Shinobu area, there is a rock about twelve feet square, supposedly the one in the legend of pattern-rubbing.[59] It is said that in ancient times a woman's love was tranformed into this rock, resulting in unique designs on its surface. Dyeing cloth on it with wild indigo generates chaotic patterns, and so many poems associate them with love. But now it lies buried in the valley, face into the ground, with nothing poetic to be seen. And yet I can't help thinking of the past, filled with longing.

planting seedlings
    with the hands—ancient patterns
    from the fern of longing
sanae toru / temoto ya mukashi / shinobuzuri

Fifth Month, 1689

* * *

PREFACE TO "RAIN HAT ISLAND"

We were told that the grave of Middle Captain Sanekata[60] was in a place called Kasashima, "Rain Hat Island," in the Natori region of Michinoku. Here Saigyō wrote of plume grass in withered fields, and with so many sorrows gathering, I felt the pathos deeply. I have longed to visit this place, but the summer rains had been pouring down and the roads were in terrible shape, so we had no choice but to pass on without seeing it.

Rain Hat Island—
    where is it this rainy month
    along muddy roads?
kasashima ya / izuko satsuki no / nukarimichi

Fifth Month, 1689

* * *

MATSUSHIMA

It's been said that Matsushima has the most splendid scenery in our land of beauty. Past and present, people with artistic minds have been enthralled with these islands, exhausting their hearts and setting their skill in motion. The sea here is about three leagues, with islands upon islands of various shapes and sizes, as if it were the wondrous carving of heaven's artistry, so fascinating and fresh. Each single pine is flourishing, all so lovely, gorgeous, beyond words.

islands and islands—
    shattered into a thousand pieces,
        summer's sea
shimajima ya / chiji ni kudakete / natsu no umi

Fifth Month, 1689

* * *

MEMORIAL FOR HIGH PRIEST TENYŪ

High Priest Tenyū, who served as a ritual specialist at Mount Haguro, is known for his power in esoteric disciplines and his merit in the dharma. He calmed his mind, broke free from thoughts, realized the ultimate reality of all phenomena, achieved perfect enlightenment. He also applied his wisdom to everyday affairs, endeavoring to bring salvation to the people. He bored out mountains and broke open rocks, working like China's great spirit of the river and the deity Joka, who had the head of a woman and the body of a snake. He built lodgings for monks, created stone steps, collected drops of moisture from the foggy mountain air, and sent it far away through a water pipe. With utensils made from rock and crafts made of wood, he made the mountain a rare jewel. Every person on Mount Haguro praises his name and reveres his virtue. Truly, High Priest Tenyū is credited for opening Mount Haguro a second time.

However, what heavenly disaster struck? There was news that he passed away, as brief as dew on a sea route, his body made to float on a breeze in the far sea of Izu. At that time, I was staying at this mountain during a pilgrimage through the three mountains of Dewa. The late High Priest's disciples encouraged me to dedicate a poem of mourning to him, and so, incompetent as I am, I made this clumsy verse which I offered up after burning incense, feeling the deepest reverence.

his jewel-like spirit—
    it returns to Mount Haguro,
        moon of the law
sono tama ya / haguro ni kaesu / nori no tsuki

Sixth Month, 1689

* * *

PREFACE TO SILVER RIVER

On a pilgrimage along the Northern Road I stayed over at a place called Izumo Point. Sado Island is off across the blue waves some eighteen leagues, lying sideways thirty-five leagues east to west. From the precipices of the peak to every corner of the valleys, it all appeared so vividly I thought I could reach out and touch it. The island has yielded great quantities of gold and has been known widely as a jewel of the world, an auspicious island, yet all types of criminals and traitors have been exiled there and now it is a shudderingly fearful place, so unfortunate. I push open my window, hoping to soothe for a time the sorrows of the road. Already the sun has sunk into the sea, the moon is dim, and the Silver River hangs across the heavens, stars glistening in cold clarity. As the sound of waves is carried in from out at sea, my spirit seems slashed, my bowels torn apart, leaving utter desolation. I can take no ease on my pillow, and my ink-black sleeves are wringing wet with tears.

> stormy sea—
> stretching out over Sado,
> Heaven's River
> *araumi ya / sado ni yokotau / ama no gawa*

Seventh Month, 1689

* * *

IN PRAISE OF A HOT SPRING

I traveled along the beach of the northern sea and bathed at the hot spring in the mountains of Kaga Province. According to the people of the area, this is one of the three famous places in Japan. As I enter the bath, the water soaks my flesh and penetrates to my muscles and bones. My heart relaxes and I feel a fresh luster in my face. It's a separate universe, a paradise cut off from the floating world, like the legendary Peach Blossom Spring. There is no need to prepare a boat and travel to Peach Blossom Spring, for there is without doubt perpetual youth and longevity of life if you enter this hot spring. It is not necessary to pick a chrysanthemum and drink the dew as Kikujido did.

> Yamanaka—
> no need to pluck chrysanthemums:
> the fragrance of these springs
> *yamanaka ya / kiku wa taoranu / yu no nio*

Summer 1689

* * *

IN TSURUGA

Second year of Genroku
On the 14th of Eighth Month, I sought lodging at Tsuruga Harbor,[61] and in the evening worshipped at the Kei Shrine. Long ago the Second Yugyō Shonin, wanting to reclaim the bog, hauled sand over here all by himself. In order to commemorate this divine deed, the practice of carrying sand has been ritually handed down to the present generation. With the holiness of the shrine and the moon's light pouring down through the trees, a deep sense of reverence seeped into my bones.

> the moon so pure
> on the sand carried here
> by the Pilgrim Priests[62]
> *tsuki kiyoshi / yugyō no moteru / tsuna no ue*

Rain fell on the 15th of the month

> harvest moon—
> the north country weather
> so uncertain
> *meigetsu ya / hokkoku biyori / sadamenaki*

On the same night, the innkeeper told us a story. "There's a temple bell deep in the sea. Once the provincial governor sent divers to search for it. And they found it, but it was upside down, so there was no way they could pull it up."

where's the moon?
the temple bell sunk
to the bottom of the sea
tsuki izuku / kane wa shizumeru / umi no soko

Afloat on a boat by Color Beach

drop your little petals,
bush clover, on the little red shells:
our little cup
kohagi chire / masuho no kogai / kosakazuki

Visiting a temple on the bay

loneliness—
superior even than Suma,
autumn on this beach[63]
sabishisa ya / suma ni kachitaru / hama no aki

Eighth Month, 1689

* * *

AKECHI'S WIFE

I stayed over at the house of Yūgen in the Ise Province. His wife was in complete accord with the wishes of her husband, faithful in every way, and she soothed a traveler's weary heart. When Akechi[64] fell into poverty, his wife cut her hair so she could prepare a renga gathering. Recalling now her selfless nature,

moon, be lonely—
I want to tell of
Akechi's wife
tsuki sabi yo / akechi ga tsuma no / hanashi sen

Ninth Month, 1689

* * *

AN ACCOUNT OF PURE WASHED HALL

Mountains are still and cultivate one's nature; water moves and consoles the feelings. There is a person who makes his dwelling between tranquillity and movement. His name is Hamada Chinseki. With his eyes he takes in all of the scenery. With his mouth he gives voice to aesthetic creativity. He clears himself of impurities and washes away the dust of the world, and so his dwelling is called Pure Washed Hall. He displays a precept banner at his gate which reads "Discrimination is not permitted to enter through this gate"—an intriguing advance on Sōkan's playful verse of instruction.[65] In his two simple ten foot square rooms he continues the rustic simplicity of Rikyū and Jōō, but he pays no heed to formal regulations. He plants trees and arranges rocks, taking these as his pleasures in a temporary world.

At Omono Bay, Seta and Karasaki extend to the right and left like two sleeves which embrace Lake Biwa and face Mikamiyama. Because the lake resembles the shape of a *biwa*, the echoing pine wind creates music with the waves. Looking up at an angle one can see Mount Hiei and the high peak of Mount Hira, with Mount Otoha and Ishiyama located behind as shoulders. Mount Nagara is arrayed with spring blossoms like hair, and Mirror Mountain adorns the autumn moon. The view changes like a lady's make-up from pale to dark day by day.[66] The wind and clouds of Chinseki's creative heart surely follows such a scene.

from the four directions,
    blossoms are blowing in:
        waves of the grebe
shihō yori / hana fukiirete / nio no nami

Third Month, 1690

* * *

WORDS FOR THE BROKEN PESTLE MALLET

That which is called a Broken Pestle is prized by those of high status as an exceptionally fine, rare jewel of our country. From out of what mountain were you born? From what village did some humble woman use you on a fulling block? Of old you were a *yokozuchi*, an ancient fulling hammer. Now you have become a flower vase, hung over the heads of the well-to-do. The nobility is like this. Even though you are from a high position, you should not swagger. Even though your rank is low, you should not resent the world. Those in the world share the fate of this fulling hammer.

> This mallet—
> long ago was it a camellia?
> a plum tree?
> *kono tsuchi no / mukashi tsubaki ka / ume no ki ka*

> Fourth Month, 1690? 1691?

* * *

AN ACCOUNT OF THE UNREAL DWELLING

In the depths of Ishiyama, behind Mount Iwama, is a mountain called Kokubu. The name apparently derives from the Kokubunji Temple located there in the distant past. Crossing the narrow stream that runs along the foot of the mountain and climbing up the path—switchbacking three times, two hundred paces in all—you come upon Hachiman Shrine. The sacred object there is a statue of the Buddha Amida. Its presence in the shrine would be quite abhorrent to the Yuiitsu School, but it's so admirable that here, as the Ryōbu School[67] holds, the Buddha dims his light and brings his blessings to the dusty world.

Usually few worshippers come, and the place emanates a deep holiness and tranquillity. Off to the side is an abandoned grass hut. Mugwort and ground bamboo engulf the eaves, the roof leaks and the plaster is crumbling off, and it has become the lair of foxes and badgers. Its name is the Unreal Dwelling. The owner was a certain monk, the uncle of the great warrior Suganuma Kyokusui. He lived here until eight years ago; now all that remains of him is his name, Old Man of the Unreal Dwelling.

I too abandoned life in the city ten years ago; now I'm nearly fifty. I am a bagworm that has lost its bag, a snail with no shell. I scorched my face in the hot sun of Kisagata in the deep north, where I wore out my heels on the jagged beaches of the northern sea along the painful dunes. Now I float on the waves of Lake Biwa. A grebe alighting its drifting nest in the shade of a single reed, I have rethatched the eaves of this hut and repaired the fences. Early in Fourth Month I happened to enter this mountain; now I wonder if I'll ever leave.

Spring departed not long ago, with azaleas still blooming and mountain wisteria hanging in the pines. From time to time a cuckoo flies by, jays bring their tidings, and even the drumming of the woodpecker isn't annoying, it's rather pleasing. My spirit rushes off southeast to Wu and Chu; my body stands at the Xiao and Xiang Rivers and Lake Dongting. To the southwest the mountain soars, off a good ways from any houses. A fragrant southern breeze descends from the peak, while the northern wind blows cool and damp from across the lake. From Mount Hie and the high peaks of Hira, the pines of Karasaki are enveloped in haze, and there is a castle, a bridge,[68] and boats with fishing lines dangling. I can hear the voice of a woodcutter heading to Mount Kasatori, the songs of seedling planters in the small rice paddies at the foot of the mountain, and the tapping of the water rail through a darkening sky sparkling with fireflies. There is certainly no lack of lovely scenes. Among them is Mount Mikami is shaped like Fuji and calls to mind my old home in Musashino, while Mount Tanakami[69] makes me think of all the Ancients whose remains are there. Other mountains are here too: Sasaho, Senjō, and Hakamagoshi. The village of Black Harbor is dark with foliage, and those tending the wicker fish weirs look just like those depicted in the *Man'yōshū*.[70]

In order to get a more expansive prospect, I clambered up the peak behind and built a platform in the pines, complete with a round straw mat. "Monkey's Perch," I call it. But I'm not a Xu Juan who built a nest in a crab apple, or an Old Wang who patched together a hermitage atop Jupu Peak. I'm just an indolent mountain dweller who stretches out his legs from steep cliffs, crushing lice in the empty mountains. Now and then when I am feeling spry, I'll scoop some pure water from the valley and cook a meal. I feel the loneliness of the trickling of the spring;[71] I live simply with nothing but a single stove. The one who lived here before was noble in spirit and devoid of

worldly artifice. Besides the room with a Buddha altar, there is
only a space to store bedding.

Not long ago the High Priest at Mount Kōra in Tsukushi,
the son of a man named Kai of the Kamo Shrine, journeyed up
to the capital, and I had someone request a calligraphy plaque
for me. Happy to oblige, he put ink to his brush and stroked the
characters for Unreal Dwelling, sending it on to me. Now it is a
keepsake for this grass hut. A mountain retreat, a traveler's rest,
it's certainly no place to build a cache of things. A cypress hat
from Kiso and a sedge raincoat from Koshi are all that hang on
the pillar above my pillow.

During the day visitors provide distraction: the old man
who looks after the shrine or some village men with farmer
stories I've never heard before, of a wild boar ravaging the rice
or rabbits getting into the bean fields. As the sun sinks past the
mountain rim, I sit into the evening quietly awaiting the moon,
my shadow as my companion, and with the lamp lit, I muse
with the penumbra over right and wrong.[72]

But with all that said, it's not that I'm utterly devoted to
solitude, hiding my traces in mountains and meadows. I'm just
a man of poor health weary of the world. I think back on the
months and years that have passed away, all the mistakes of my
stumbling life. At one point I coveted a government position
with a fief of land. Another time I longed to enter the precincts
of the Buddha and the halls of the patriarchs. But I've kept tormenting my body as I drift like a windblown cloud, struggling
over feelings about flowers and birds, thinking I might make my
living this way. In the end, devoid of talent or skill, I cling to this
one thread. For its sake Bo Juyi exhausted the vitality of his five
organs, and Du Fu wasted away. In wisdom or artistry I am no
match for them, yet isn't it true that there's no place that's not
an unreal dwelling, thoughts I now abandon as I head to bed.

> for now I'll rely
> on the pasania tree:
> summer grove
> *mazu tanomu / shii no ki mo ari / natsu kodachi*

Seventh Month, 1690

* * *

PROSE POEM ON THE UNREAL DWELLING

This body, nearly fifty now, has become an aged tree with bitter peaches, a snail that has lost its shell, a bagworm without its bag, drifting along on the aimless wind. Sōkan put up with wayfarer's meals morning and night, and Nōin sought alms for his mendicant's purse. I scorched my face at Matsushima and Shirakawa, and my tears soaked my sleeves at Holy Mount Yudono. I yearned to make it to the shores where puffins cry and gaze upon the Thousand Islands of the Ainu, but my companion Sora held me back with worries about my frail health, and I relented. I ventured instead to the place called Kisagata, where I wore out my heels on the jagged beaches of the northern sea along the painful dunes. Now this year, I float on the waves of Lake Biwa, a grebe in its drifting nest seeking lodging by the single shaft of a reed.

My place is known as the Unreal Dwelling, by the mountain Kokubu. An ancient shrine is nearby, purifying my six senses, all trace of dust fallen away. This deserted grass hut is where the uncle of the warrior Suganuma lived, having abandoned the world. He passed on eight years ago; the hut remains at the crossroads of unreality. Truly enlightenment and delusion are resolved in this one word, unreality,[73] and it is impossible to forget for an instant the fleeting impermanence of life.

These are not deep mountains, but the houses stand far apart. Ishiyama faces my hut, with Mount Iwama rising behind. A fragrant southern breeze descends from the peak, while the northern wind blows cool and damp from across the lake. I arrived early in Fourth Month, with azaleas still blooming and mountain wisteria hanging in the pines. From time to time a cuckoo flies by, jays bring their tidings, and even the drumming of the woodpecker isn't annoying. "Mountain cuckoo, make me feel loneliness"[74]—such is my joy in solitude, such spontaneous delight. Compared to China's famed Wu and Chu, this scene has nothing to be ashamed of. It is hardly inferior to the Five Lakes and Three Bays.

From Mount Hie and the high peaks of Hira, the pines of Karasaki are enveloped in haze. The castle at Zeze gleams among the trees, and the light of the setting sun lingers on Seta Bridge, connecting to the pine grove at Awazu. Mount Mikami is shaped like Fuji and calls to mind my old hut at Musashino, and Mount Tanakami brings forth deep feeling for the Ancients whose remains are there. Other mountains are here too: Sasaho, Senjō, and Hakamagoshi. And there is the peculiar legend that the villagers of Black Harbor are dark because they have not taken bamboo hats from Kasatori Mountain.

In order to get a more expansive prospect, I clambered up the peak behind and built a platform in the pines, complete with a round straw mat. "Monkey's Perch," I call it. Xu Juan built a nest in a crab apple where he drank with friends, but that was in a city, and I have no reason to covet the hermitage Old Wang patched together atop Jupu Peak. My eyes opened to emptiness, I just sit on this steep mountain crushing lice.

At times when I feel lively I gather firewood and scoop water from a spring. I feel the loneliness of the trickling spring that drips along the green of the ferns. I live simply with nothing but a single stove. The man who dwelled here before was noble in spirit and shunned baubles. Besides the room with a Buddha altar, there is only a space to store bedding.

Not long ago the High Priest of Rendai-in at Mount Kōra journeyed up to the capital, and I had someone request a calligraphy plaque for me. Happy to oblige, he took up his brush and stroked the characters for Unreal Dwelling, sending it on to me. On the back, he wrote his name to serve as a keepsake for those who come later. A mountain retreat, a traveler's rest, this is certainly no place to build a cache of things. A cypress hat from Kiso and a sedge raincoat from Koshi are all that hang on the pillar above my pillow.

During the day, the old man who looks after the shrine may stop by or some elderly men from the village with tales of a wild boar ravaging the rice or rabbits getting into the bean fields, stories I've never heard before. And in the rare occasion visitors come here, we sit quietly into the night with our shadows as companion, musing with the penumbra over right and wrong.

But with all that said, it's not that I'm utterly devoted to solitude, hiding my traces in mountains and meadows. I'm just a man of poor health weary of the world. What can I say? I have not practiced the dharma life. I have not followed worldly pursuits. I've been fond of my eccentricities ever since I was quite

young and I thought I'd make my living that way for a time.
Now I've come to cling to this one thread, ashamed of my lack
of talent or skill. I toil in vain, my spirit worn out, my brow
wrinkled. Early autumn is half over, dawn and dusk transform the
scenes—surely this is dwelling in unreality. And with that I rise
and leave.

Seventh Month, 1690

* * *

THE EVENING COOL AT RIVERSIDE, FOURTH AVENUE

"The evening cool at riverside, Fourth Avenue," they call it.
From early Sixth Month with its evening moon, to the moon at
dawn just past mid-month, people line up along the river in
platforms drinking sake and feasting as they party all night
long. Women wrapped in showy sashes, men sporting fashion-
ably long coats, with monks and old folks intermingling, even
apprentices to coopers and blacksmiths, everyone carefree and
leisurely, singing up a storm. Yes, indeed, life in the capital!

> river breeze—
> wearing pale persimmon robes,
> the evening cool
> *kawakaze ya / usugaki kitaru / yūsuzumi*

Summer, 1690

* * *

ON A PORTRAIT BY UNCHIKU

Unchiku,[75] a monk in Kyōto, painted a picture—perhaps a self-
portrait—of a monk with his face turned away. He asked me to
add a legend to it, so I wrote: You are over sixty, and I nearly
fifty. Together in a dream, we present the forms of dreams. Here
I add the words of one asleep:

turn this way:
I too am lonely;
    autumn evening
kochira muke / ware mo sabishiki / aki no kure

Autumn, 1690

* * *

ON A PORTRAIT OF SOTOBA KOMACHI[76]

Ah, admirable, admirable! The bamboo hat is admirable. The straw coat is admirable. What kind of person bestows this to us, what person makes such a painting, this vision from a thousand years, appearing right here? Now with this form, the spirit too appears. The coat so admirable, the hat so admirable.

so admirable—
    even on a day without snow,
        straw coat and bamboo hat[77]
tōtosa ya / yuki furanu hi mo / mino to kasa

Responding to a request from Jōkō Ajiyari.

Winter, 1690–91

* * *

RECORD OF THE VILLA OF FALLEN PERSIMMONS

A man from Kyōto by the name of Kyorai has a cottage in a grove of bamboo, in lower Saga at the foot of Mount Arashi by the Ōi River. It is a place for lonely tranquillity, where the heart comes clear. This Kyorai is so lazy: weeds grow high outside his window, the branches of persimmon trees hang long over everything, the summer rains leak in all over, the tatami mats and paper screens are rank with mold, and there's no good place to sleep. And particularly the shade: such generous hospitality from the host.

summer rains—
    poetry cards peeled off,
        their traces on the wall
    samidare ya / shikishi hegitaru / kabe no ato

                                    Summer, 1691

                * * *

ON THE NIGHT OF THE 16TH AT KATADA BAY

The excitement from last night's full moon had not quieted
down when, encouraged by two or three friends, we set off by
boat to Katada Bay. About four in the afternoon of that day, we
arrived at the back of the house of a certain Moee Narihide. We
all called out, "These old drunks of wild words have been enjoying the moon and now we're here." Narihide had not expected
us and was surprised and delighted. He rolled up his blinds and
swept away the dust. He said, "In my garden are only potatoes
and black-eyed peas. The carp we have is prepared poorly, so
there is nothing interesting to offer you." Then he spread out
straw mats at the beach and treated us to a party. Before waiting long the moon rose, shining vividly on the lake. I had heard
that at exactly mid-autumn, the full moon rises directly above a
mountain facing the Floating Temple, and so the mountain has
come to be called Mirror Mountain.

Looking out from the ballustrade atop this hall, we saw
that the moon of that night was not far from where it rose the
day before. I could see Mount Mikami and Muzukuki Hill to
the south and north. Between them extended small hills with
numerous peaks clustered together. The moon, by then high in
the sky, became hidden in black clouds, and I couldn't distinguish which was Mirror Mountain. Showing his wholehearted
hospitality, the master quoted Saigyō, "It is precisely when, from
time to time, that the clouds hide the moon. . . ."[78]

Finally the moon broke off from the clouds and with the
golden wind and silver waves, it was reflected in the light of the
thousand-form Buddha. "Is it only the declining moon that is
regrettable?" I said, taking up Teika's sigh. We can compare the

sky of the 16th night to the world as a way of realizing the impermanence of life. "It's precisely because he visited here that the high priest Eshin wet his sleeves with tears," our host said. As we prepared to leave he said, "But you've come all this way to enjoy this scene, how can I let you leave with low spirits?" So we raised our cups on the shore as the moon was about to reach Yokawa valley in the depths of Mount Hiei.

> open the lock
>   let the moon shine in—
>   Floating Temple
> *jō akete / tsuki sashireyo / ukimidō*

> how easily it rose
>   and now it hesitates,
>   the moon in clouds
> *yasuyasu to / idete izayou / tsuki no kumo*

Eighth Month, 1691

* * *

WORDS IN PRAISE OF THE PINE OF NARIHIDE'S GARDEN

There is a pine here reaching to nine feet. The lower branches extend over ten feet, growing on top of each other thick with needles. The wind plucks the koto pine, calling forth rain, giving rise to waves. The sound resembles a lute, a flute, and a drum, and the waves blend with the echoes of heaven.

At the present time there is a man who loves peonies, collecting unusual ones and full of boasting. And there is another man who raises chrysanthemums, competing with others and laughing at their small blossoms. A person who raises persimmon trees and various kinds of citrus considers only their fruit, paying no heed to the shape of their branches and leaves. The pine alone remains verdant after the frost, staying unchanged through the four seasons, and yet the charm of its appearance shifts through the year. Bo Juyi said, "The pine exhales the old qi[79] so it is preserved for a thousand years." The pine brings joy

to the master's eyes and consolation to his heart. But not only
this, for having learned the *qi* of preserving life and health, he
will surely pledge to wait out his old age with the pine.

＊ ＊ ＊   Eighth Month, 1691

AMIDABŌ

Brushwood hut:
    the words sound
        so despicable and yet
in this world it is
    a thing of true delight
shiba no io / to kikeba iyashiki / nanaredomo /
yo ni konomoshiki / mono ni zo arikeru

This poem, included in the *Sankashū*, was written by the
Priest Saigyō when he visited a monk named Amidabō living in
the Higashiyama district of Kyōto. I delight in wondering what
kind of person that monk was. Here I offer a poem to a monk
who now spends his life in a grass hut.

the brushwood hut's
    moon—just as it was
        for Amidabō
shiba no to no / tsuki ya sonomama / amidabō

                                        Autumn, 1691

＊ ＊ ＊

STAYING OVER AT RIYŪ'S PLACE AT MENSHŌ TEMPLE

Fourth year of Genroku, Tenth Month
    It has been a hundred years since this temple was moved
here from the village of Hirata. As it says in the record of con-
tributions for the temple, "Bamboo and trees grow densely, and

the earth and rocks are aged with moss." A truly venerable grove, deeply moving in its aura of great age.

> the ambience
> of a hundred years: this garden's
> fallen leaves
> *momotose no / keshiki o niwa no / ochiba kana*

Tenth Month, 1691

* * *

EARLY WINTER SHOWER AT SHIMADA

As early winter showers fell desolately, I sought a night's lodging. I dried my wet clothes by the hearth fire and scooped water to my mouth. The master of the inn treated me with kindness, comforting for a while the troubles of my journey. As the day ended, I laid down under the lamp, took out my ink and brush set, and started to write. Noticing this, he earnestly asked for a poem to remember our one moment of meeting.

> putting up at an inn
> I am asked my name:
> early winter shower
> *yado karite / na o nanorasuru / shigure kana*

Tenth Month, 1691

* * *

WITHERED MISCANTHUS IN SNOW

With no settled place in this world, for the last six or seven years I've spent my nights on the road, suffering many illnesses. Unable to forget dear friends and disciples of many years, I finally made my way back to the Musashi Plain.[80] Day after day they have come to visit my poor hut, and I offer this verse in reply:

somehow
  still alive—snow on
    withered miscanthus
    tomokakumo / narade ya yuki no / kareobana

Eleventh Month, 1691

* * *

WORDS ON LEAVING THE NEST

After rambling around here and there, I holed up for the winter at a place called Tachibana, passing First and Second Months there. Meditating on my art, I've reached the point of saying "enough of this" and tried to muffle the voice of poetry. But poetic feelings keep luring me on, and something is always flickering in my mind. Poetry has become my daemon. Now I've abandoned everything and left my old nest; with but a few coins in my pocket, I've entrusted my life to a mendicant's staff and bowl. And so this is what has become of me, clothed in a beggar's coat of straw.

Second Month, 1692

* * *

WORDS ON TRANSPLANTING A *BASHŌ* TREE (1)

Chrysanthemums flourished by Tao Yuanming's eastern fence, and bamboos became Wang Shiyu's friend outside his north window. Peonies give rise to arguments of "this" or "that," staining them with the dusty world. Lotus leaves don't grow in common ground; if the water is clear they simply won't bloom.

    What year was it when I moved my little nest into this area and planted that solitary *bashō* tree? Perhaps the climate agrees with it, because many trunks have sprung up, their leaves growing densely, shrinking my garden and overhanging my eaves. And so people have come to name my hut after this plant. Old friends and disciples alike are fond of it, taking cuttings of the buds or dividing the roots, carrying them to this place and that, year after year.

One year I set my heart on a pilgrimage to the north country, abandoning this Bashō Hut. The tree wandered to places beyond my bamboo fence, my neighbors repeatedly seeking it out as protection from frost and wind. A concern that "the pine would be left all alone" grew in my heart, and all the farewells of my journey with my regret at leaving the tree brought surprising sorrow—five springs and autumns have gone by this way. Here once again at the *bashō* tree, my sleeves are soaked with tears. Now in the middle of the fifth year of Genroku, the fragrance of the orange tree is not far away and the closeness of friends is unchanged: there's no way I'd leave again.

The site of my former hut is nearby, and this little thatched cottage, with but three rooms, suits me well. The cryptomeria pillars are well hewn, the bamboo wicket gate is tranquil, the reed fence provides a sturdy enclosure, and it faces south toward a pond like a tower overlooking a lake. The land itself looks out on Mount Fuji and by the brushwood gate is an oblique but unobstructed view. Like the Zhe River in China, the divided river at Mitsumatsu is superb for moonviewing. Since the crescent moon first appeared, I've been fretful when clouds would come, distressed at the possibility of rain. In order to enhance the beauty of the moon, *bashō* trees have been transplanted. The leaves are over seven feet long, and they rip halfway to midrib in the wind, as painful as a phoenix's broken tail, as poigniant as a torn green fan. Occasionally it will bloom, but the flowers are unimpressive; the stalk is thick, but no axe bothers with it. Like that useless tree in the mountains, it has an admirable nature. The monk Huaisu ran his brush along it; Zhang Hengshu gained strength for his studies just by gazing upon the emerging leaves. But I'm not like those two. I just relax in the shade of these leaves, loving the way they tear so easily.

Autumn, 1692

* * *

WORDS ON TRANSPLANTING A *BASHŌ* TREE (2)

Admirable it is for the heart to be wholly empty. To be free of skill and knowledge is true realization. Then come wayfarers who are liberated from any house or home. But the iron will required for true detachment is too much for the wings of some little dove.[81]

One time, as if swept up by a sudden wind, I wore out my cypress hat far into the north country.[82] Now three years have passed, and once again I am back here just east of the river in Edo, feeling the sorrow of autumn where an island divides the waters, tears streaming over the yellow chrysanthemums of bygone days.[83] Sanpū and Kifū have shown their kindness by building this hut; Sora and Taisui have tinged it with austere beauty. Its back to the north, it is protected from winter; facing south, it allows in the evening cool. Bamboo handrails face out on the pond, most likely for the benefit of moonviewers. Since the crescent moon first appeared, I've been fretful when clouds would come, distressed at the possibility of rain.

People have sent over numerous items, keeping my gourd overflowing with rice and my bottle filled with sake. Bamboo are planted all around and I'm surrounded by trees, so I feel as if I'm in deep seclusion. In order to enhance the beauty of the moon, five *bashō* trees have been planted. The leaves are over seven feet long and could cover a *koto* or be sewn into a case for a *biwa*. They wave in the wind like a phoenix's tail and tear in the rain like a green dragon's ears. Day by day the rolled-up new leaves grow like Master Hengqu's view of learning; they open out as if awaiting the brush of Saint Shaonien. But I'm not like these two. I just relax in the shade of these leaves, loving the way they tear so easily.

> banana leaves
> will hang by the pillars:
> moon over the hut
> *bashōba o / hashira ni kaken / io no tsuki*

Autumn, 1692

* * *

FAREWELL TO TŌZAN

Tōzan spent three months in Edo on account of his work. I would visit him in the morning and surprise him while he was still sleeping. He would visit me at night and wake me after I had gone to bed. And so visiting and being visited, we got to know each other as well as if we shared food and slept under the same roof.

Today at last he returned home. I went to see him off, and he headed off drawing his staff uncertainly. Around us autumn was coming to an end, and his departure, along with departing autumn, was deeply regrettable.

> Musashino fields—
> no hindrances now,
> your bamboo hat
> *musashino ya / sawaru mono naki / kimi ga kasa*

Autumn, 1692? 1693?

* * *

IN PRAISE OF A DESK

In moments of leisure, I lean my elbow on it, and forgetting myself and breathing deeply, I cultivate my *qi*. In quiet times I open a book and search for the spirit in the sage's mind and the wiseman's genius. In moments of tranquillity I take out my brush, entering the inner heart of Wang Xizi and Huai Su. And so this skillfully made desk is one thing but has three uses. Its height is eight inches, its surface two feet wide. On its two supports are carved the divination trigrams of Heaven and Earth. I learn from the virtues of the hidden dragon and the female horse. And so I wonder, should I consider this one function or two?

In response to an inquiry from Ranshi, mid-winter, Genroku period.

Winter, 1692–93

* * *

PRAISE FOR A PAINTING OF THREE SAGES

Now, for those who set their heart on the spiritual arts[84] and follow the four seasons, writing is as inexhaustible as the sands on the beach. Those who can express the sentiments of nature, being in touch with the subtle feelings in things, are the masters[85] of literature.

In the Bunmei era the aesthetic Way flourished with the words of master poets, writings that are now our model. The joy of continuing their truth is difficult for those today. However, the currents of aesthetic creativity shift along with Heaven and Earth, inexhaustible change that is so precious. And so, desiring a portrait of Sōgi, Sōkan, and Moritake, I sought out the brush work of Kyoriku, a man accomplished in the aesthetic Way. I have added a clumsy verse to this portraits and now I can only bow to them with prayers that the Way flourish forever.

> these three
> of the moon and flowers—
> masters of the truth
> *tsuki hana no / kore ya makoto no / arujitachi*

Summer, 1693

* * *

WORDS OF FAREWELL TO KYORIKU

Just last autumn I happened to meet him, only to lament his departure now at the beginning of Fifth Month. As our separation approached, he knocked on the door of my grass hut, and we talked leisurely all day long. Richly talented, he loves both painting and poetry, and I thought I'd assay his interests. "Why are you fond of painting?" I asked. "Because of poetry," he replied. "Why do you love poetry?" "Because of painting." Thus, these two arts have one use. Yes, "It is shameful for a gentleman to have many accomplishments,"[86] so turning two arts to one purpose is praiseworthy indeed. In painting he is my teacher; in poetry I instruct him and he is my disciple. My teacher has penetrated the spiritual depths of painting and his brush moves with wondrous subtlety. I cannot take in all the mysterious profundity of his works.

I offered these words to him: "My poetry is like a stove in summer or a fan in winter. It runs counter to popular tastes; it is of no practical use. But even in trifling words tossed off by Shunzei[87] and Saigyō, there is much that is moving. Hasn't retired Emperor Go-Toba[88] stated, 'In their poetry is truth, suffused with sorrow.' Gain strength from these words; do not stray from this one thin thread. In Kūkai's writings we find, 'Do not follow in the footsteps of the Ancients; seek what they sought.' This is true also of *haikai* poetry." I lifted my lantern. I walked with him just past the gate. And then he departed.

Sixth Month, 1693

* * *

WORDS SENT TO KYORIKU

The man returning to his native village along the Kiso Road is named Morikawa Kyoriku. From olden times, those drawn deeply to the poetic way hoisted packs on their backs and suffered the pains of straw sandals, with torn hats as their protection against frost and dew. Disciplining their hearts, they attained the truth of things, their greatest joy. Now, in order to serve his lord, Kyoriku slings a sword at his hip, and behind his pack horse march a spearman and young retainer, their black robes waving in the wind. Surely this is not his true nature.

> emulate the heart
>   of pasania blossoms:
>   a Kiso journey
> *shii no hana no / kokoro ni mo niyo / kiso no tabi*

> learn from the journey
>   of a sorrowing wayfarer:
>   flies of Kiso
> *uki hito no / tabi ni mo narae / kiso no hae*

Fifth month, 1693

* * *

AN EXPLANATION OF SECLUSION

Sexual passion is despised by the Confucian gentleman, and it is the first prohibition[89] in Buddhism's Five Precepts, yet it is so difficult to discard and often involves deep feelings. Vows get made under evening plum trees of Mount Kurabu,[90] unseen by others, then unexpectedly one is taken over by the scent of love. Among the hidden hills, with no one watching over, indiscretions occur. There are countless examples of people drowning in desire for a daughter of the shore,[91] selling one's house and ruining one's life. But craving a long life and tormenting one's spirit on worldly desires is to lack sensitivity to life. Compared to these, the sins of lovers are slight and tolerable.

It is rare for anyone to reach the age of seventy, and the period when mind and body truly flourish is not much more than twenty years. The span of our first forty years, after which old age sets in, is like the dream of a single night. At fifty or sixty, we begin to sink into infirmity and grow increasingly pathetic. In the evening, we tire prematurely then awake early in the morning, not knowing what we want to do.

Fools have many worries. Those who amass carnal desires and then excel in some art are unsurpassed in distinguishing right and wrong. But for some who make art their vocation become enraged at the demonic world of avarice only to end up drowning in a field-side ditch, unable to sustain their art. As the Old Sage of the Southern Flower[92] said, abandon pros and cons, forget youth and old age, and live in tranquillity: this is the delight of an old man.

When someone comes by, there is useless chatter. When I visit others, I worry that I'm disturbing them. Sun Jing shut his door; Du Wulang locked his gate.[93] Having no friends will be my true friend; poverty will be my wealth. An obstinate old man of fifty years, I write to admonish myself.

> morning glories—
> locked during daytime,
> my fence gate
> *asagao ya / hiru wa jō orosu / mon no kaki*

Autumn, 1693

* * *

THE LIFE OF TŌJUN

The venerable Tōjun[94] was of the Enomoto family, and his grandfather, named Takeshita, was an eminent farmer from Katada in Gōshū. The Enomotos are from Kikaku's maternal family line. This year at the age of seventy-two, he gazed upon the autumn moon from his sickbed. With affection for birds and flowers and sadness at the sight of dew, his spirit remained unruffled even as he lay on his deathbed. Finally, as a keepsake he left behind a *hokku* on Sarashina and then passed away upheld by the power of the Lotus Sutra. After studying medicine when he was young, it became his career. With a stipend from Lord Honda, no dust gathered in his cooking pot.[95] But he loathed worldly life and eventually cast off the trappings of his profession, breaking his doctor's staff and abandoning his work. He was in his early sixties. Turning his city residence into a mountain retreat, he lived in delight, and for over ten years he neither put down his brush nor left his desk. So prolific were his writings that they would overflow from a cart. Born by a lake, he met his end in the eastern plain. Surely he was "a great hermit in the middle of a city."

> the moon has set;
>   all that remains is
>   the four corners of his desk
> *iru tsuki no / ato wa tsukue no / yosumi kana*

Autumn, 1693

* * *

VISITING SODŌ'S CHRYSANTHEMUM GARDEN

Sixth year of Genroku, 9th day of the first month of winter, visiting Sodō's chrysanthemum garden.

The Chrysanthemum Festival is held today, the 9th day of the Tenth Month,[96] because in Ninth Month the chrysanthemums had not yet budded. As a Chinese poem[97] says, "The Chrysanthemum Festival is any time they are in bloom," and it's not unprecedented for the Festival to be postponed. So though

it's winter, we're encouraged to write poems on the autumn
chrysanthemum.

> chrysanthemum fragrance—
> in the garden, the sole
> of a worn-out sandal
> *kiku no ka ya / niwa ni kiretaru / kutsu no soko*

Winter, 1693

* * *

PREFACE TO "LIGHTNING"

At Honma Shume's[98] house, hanging on the back wall of a Nō
stage, is a portrait of skeletons playing flute and drum. Is human
life any different than the sporting of skeletons? Zhuangzi used
a skull for his pillow and didn't distinguish dream from reality[99]—truly, this evokes the character of our lives.

> lightning—
> through the face,
> miscanthus plumes[100]
> *inazuma ya / kao no tokoro ga / susuki no ho*

Sixth Month, 1694

* * *

CONSTRUCTING A HAT

Living a desolate life alone behind the door of my grass hut,
feeling the loneliness whenever autumn's wind would blow, I
borrow Myōkan's sword, and emulating the craft of the
Bamboo Cutter, I chop bamboo and bend them, and proclaim
myself, "Old Man Maker of Hats." But lacking any skill, I can
spend a whole day at this work and fail to finish a hat. Per-
turbed, as the days passed I have grown weary of the task. In the
morning I stretch paper over the bamboo; in the evening when
they were dry I put on more paper. I dye the paper in persimmon

juice and have to harden it with lacquer. Now after twenty days have passed, it is done. The rim of the hat slants inward and then outward, just like a half-opened leaf of a lotus. This peculiar shape is more appealing than one that is perfectly crafted. Is it Saigyō's hat of loneliness or the one Old Su wore under a sky of snow? Perhaps I'll journey to see the dew of Miyagi Plain, or pull my staff through the snow under Wu skies. Hurrying through hail or waiting for winter showers, I cherish this hat that gives me such delight. Suddenly a certain feeling comes over me: to be drenched once again in Sōgi's showers. So I pick up my brush and jot this down inside my hat:

> in a world of rain
>   life is like Sōgi's
>   temporary shelter[101]
> *yo ni furu mo / sarani sōgi no / yadori kana*

Date unknown (*hokku* written in 1682)

NOTES

INTRODUCTION

1. See glossary on the terms *haikai*, *haiku*, *hokku*, and *haibun*.
2. For an interpretation of this episode and its relationship to Bashō's wayfaring ideal, see my "Impermanence, Fate, and the Journey: Bashō and the Problem of Meaning," *Religion* 16 (1986): 323–341.
3. For an interpretation of this image and its significance, see my "Bashō as Bat: Wayfaring and Anti-Structure in the Journals of Matsuo Bashō (1644–1694)," *Journal of Asian Studies* 49 (1990): 274–290.
4. There are two versions that can be considered final editions of this text, and while for the most part I have followed the Japanese tradition of using the Okimori text, Donald Keene has made a strong argument for preferring the Sanpū text. See his "Bashō's Sarashina Journal," *Appreciations of Japanese Culture* (Tokyo: Kodansha, 1981), pp. 109–130. The one clear superiority of the Sanpū text is the inclusion of a line that informs the reader that when Bashō dismounted from the horse, the servant took his place—a fact only implied in the Okimori text.
5. This work is distinguished from his travel accounts not only in that he is staying in one place, but also in its structure of precisely dated entries, typical of the diary (*nikki*) but not the travel journal (*kikō*).
6. See the glossary for a brief discussion of these and other aesthetic terms.

7. For a brilliant discussion of Bashō's use of cultural associations in his experience of nature, see Haruo Shirane, *Traces of Dreams: Landscape, Cultural Memory, and the Poetry of Bashō* (Stanford, CA: Stanford University Press, 1998).

8. Keene, *Appreciations of Japanese Culture*, p. 124. Donald Keene calls the view of Bashō as a poet of nature a "misconception," stating that he "tended to see landscapes through the poetry written about them." Bashō did tend to see nature through culture, but the idea that this implies that he is not a poet of nature rests on a particular Western definition of nature.

9. To oversimplify a complex and important idea, the Creative (*zōka*) is a term for the world's unceasing and spontaneous disposition to give rise to beautiful and skillful transformations throughout the natural world. True art is a participation in nature's own creativity.

10. For a recent anthology of essays on place, as well as a bibliography of other writings about this idea, see my *At Home on the Earth: Becoming Native to our Place* (Berkeley, CA: University of California Press, 1999).

11. The other was the narrative (*monogatari*), with Lady Murasaki's *The Tale of Genji* (*Genji monogatari*, ca. 1011) the most famous example.

12. Gary Snyder, *The Back Country* (New York: New Directions, 1968); Cid Corman and Kamaike Susumu, trans. *Back Roads to Far Towns: Bashō's Oku-no-hosomichi* (New York: Mushinsha, 1968); Peter Matthiessen, *Snow Leopard* (New York: Viking, 1978); Gretel Ehrlich, *Islands, The Universe, Home* (New York: Penguin, 1991); Sam Hamill, *Bashō's Ghost* (Seattle: Broken Moon, 1989); John Elder, *Following the Brush: An American Encounter with Classical Japanese Culture* (Boston: Beacon Press, 1993); see also his *Imagining the Earth: Poetry and the Vision of Nature* (Urbana: University of Illinois Press, 1985). It is worth adding that Beat poet Lawrence Ferlinghetti titled one of his poetry collections *Back Roads to Far Places* (New York: New Directions, 1971).

13. *Matsuo Bashō shū, Nihon koten bungaku zenshū*, vol. 41 (Tokyo: Shogakkan, 1972).

14. For more details on Bashō's use of seasonal nature imagery in his poetry, see my *Bashō's Haiku: Selected Poems by Matsuo Bashō* (Albany: State University of New York Press, 2004).

CHAPTER 1.
JOURNAL OF BLEACHED BONES IN A FIELD

1. Naemuri Chiri (1648–1716) thinks back to the Fukagawa district of Edo, where Bashō's hut and its *bashō* tree were located. Mount Fuji is visible in the distance.

2. If the poem is not written by Bashō, the poet's name appears in parenthesis after the romanized version of the poem.

3. Chiri again thinks back to Edo, where friends are probably counting the days, wondering where Bashō is, and worrying about him crossing the broad and dangerous Ōi River.

4. Du Mu was a Chinese Tang poet. Bashō refers to his poem: "My whip dangling, I trust my horse; / riding mile after mile, still no cockcrow. / In the woods I drowse in dream; / then leaves fly about, and I am startled awake."

5. Bashō draws on a poem by the monk Saigyō (1118–90): "Entering deeply, / searching out the depths / of the pathway of the gods: / high above, over all, / a mountain peak with pine wind" [*fukaku irite / kamiji no oku o / tazunureba / mata ue mo naki / mine no matsukaze*].

6. The passage refers to the legend of Urashima, who rescued a turtle. In gratitude, it took him to the Dragon Palace. He spent some time there and was given a treasure box, which he was warned not to open. When he returned home he found that everything had changed, and when he opened the box, he instantly became an old man with white hair.

7. The bow was used to make soft cotton yarn, and made a sound that resembled a lute.

8. The passage refers to a story in the Chinese Daoist text *Zhuangzi*, attributed to Zhuangzi (or Chuang Tzu), in which an ancient tree is so huge that oxen can hide behind

it. In the *Zhuangzi*, the tree lives long because it is useless—thus proving the usefulness of uselessness. Bashō turns the story into a Buddhist one.

9. Clothes were pounded on a fulling block to clean and soften them, and in the poetic tradition the sound was associated with loneliness. The fulling block was not commonly used in Bashō's time, but he wishes to hear its sound in order to feel deeply what was considered the essential nature of Yoshino in autumn. There is an allusion to a poem by Fujiwara Masatsune (1170–1221): "At Yoshino / the mountain wind / deepens into the night, / and in the old village / a fulling block is struck" [*miyoshino no / yama no akikaze / sayo fukete / furusato samuku / koromo utsunari*].

10. Bashō refers to a *waka* attributed at that time to Saigyō: "By my hermitage / I draw up pure spring water / that trickles down / drop after drop without cease / between mossy rocks" [*tokutoku to / otsuru iwama no / koke shimizu / kumihosu hodo mo / naki sumai kana*]. Bashō repeats the phrase *tokutoku* three times in this passage.

11. During the Hōgen Disturbance of 1156, Yoshitomo (1123–60) fought and killed his father, Tameyoshi, the leader of the powerful Minamoto clan. Two years later he was defeated in the Heiji Disturbance and fled virtually alone to Owari Province, experiencing the cold loneliness that autumn wind suggests. Yoshitomo was assassinated in Owari, and soon after Tokiwa, his mistress, was murdered, perhaps by robbers. Arakida Moritake (1473–1549), a Shinto priest at the Ise Shrine, was one of the founders of *haikai* poetry.

12. Shinobu means both to remember and to long for. *Shinobugusa*, literally "grass of longing/remembrance," is a fern (*Polypodium lineare* or *Davallia bullata*).

13. In a popular story, Chikusai was a comical doctor who lost his patients because he kept indulging in "wild poetry." Like Chikusai, Bashō "looked very shabby" as he traveled to Nagoya, where he gave this poem to his host.

14. Karasaki, on Lake Biwa, is famous for a picturesque pine and beautiful scenery. Nearby is Mount Nagara, known for hazy cherry blossoms. Haze is traditionally associated with

spring evenings. This *hokku* alludes to a *waka* by Emperor Go-toba (1180–1239): "At Karasaki / the green of the pine / is also in haze / extending from blossoms: / spring dawn" [*karasaki no / matsu no midori mo / oboro nite / hana yori tsuzuku / haru no akebono*]. Go-toba was an accomplished *waka* poet and theorist who commissioned the great poetry anthology Shinkokinshū (1216).

CHAPTER 2. KASHIMA JOURNAL

1. Yashuara Teishitsu (1610–73), a disciple of Matsunaga Teitoku from Kyōto.
2. A popular name for Ariwara Yukihira (818–93). Teishitsu refers to his poem written during his exile in Suma: "If by chance / someone asks about me / tell them I live in loneliness / by Suma Bay, weeping / as I gather seaweed" [*wakuraba ni / tou hito araba / suma no ura ni / moshiotaretsutsu / wabu to kotae yo*].
3. Iwanami Sora (1649–1710), the disciple who would later accompany him to the Deep North.
4. A common image in East Asian Buddhism, in which the newly enlightened Buddha returns to the world to save sentient beings.
5. A Zen image for the entrance to enlightenment, as well as the title of a famous collection of koans.
6. A mountainous area in China famous for being a place in which poets and monks sought seclusion.
7. Hattori Ransetsu (1654–1707), one of the first of Bashō's disciples and considered one of the Four Worthies of the Bashō school.
8. A legendary prince of ancient Japan. A *waka* about Tsukuba attributed to him appears in the ancient text *Kojiki* (712).
9. The first anthology of *renga* poetry, compiled by Nijō Yoshimoto (1320–88), was titled the Tsukuba Anthology (*Tsukubashū*, 1356). Because of the enormous influence of this collection, *renga* was sometimes called the "Way of Tsukuba."

10. Tachibana Tamenaka (d. 1085), late Heian poet. This story is presented in the *Mumyōshū* by Kamo no Chōmei (1153–1216).

11. Alludes to a number of passages in Chinese and Japanese literature where poets passed the night amid the smell of fish.

12. The shrine had a sacred foundation stone that embodied the holiness of the kami. Dew-wet moss grew on the stone.

13. In rice harvesting season, farmers are so busy they work on moonlit nights.

14. Taro were sold during the harvest moon viewing festival of the Eighth Month.

15. Walking through a dew-drenched bush clover field might dye his trousers the rose-purple color of that plant.

16. Jijun (1623–97) was a physician living in seclusion at Itako. The three verses are the first three links of a linked-verse sequence. The first one is a greeting verse by the host, humbly welcoming his guests. The second is the principal guest, praising the host. The third has been interpreted two ways: moonviewers either seeking a ride on the tugboat (which pulls boats upriver), or asking to get off.

CHAPTER 3. KNAPSACK NOTEBOOK

1. From a passage in chapter two of the *Zhuangzi*.

2. A term Bashō made up as a pen name, literally it means "wind-gauze-priest" (*fūrabō*). It is both easily blown by the wind and torn by it (like the leaves of the *bashō* plant).

3. Refers to *haikai* poetry, which shuns traditional conventions.

4. A similar passage is found in the *haibun* "An Account of the Unreal Dwelling." In the opening passage of *Sarashina Journal*, Bashō describes himself as a "bat," in between a bird (a monk) and a mouse (man of the world).

5. Sōgi (1421–1502) was a classical *renga* poet and travel journalist. Sesshū (1420–1506) was a famous monk-painter of the Muromachi period, a master of Chinese style land-

scape ink-painting. Sen no Rikyū (1520–91) was Zen-influenced master of the Way of Tea (*chadō*) who championed the aesthetic of *wabi* (aesthetic rusticity).

6. Draws on a passage in Confucius's *Analects*: "my Way has one thread running through it."

7. An important and complex idea in Bashō's view of nature derived from the *Zhuangzi* and later Chinese philosophic and aesthetic traditions. The term refers not to nature in our normal sense of the world, but to nature's skillful creativity that beautifully transforms the natural world.

8. The classical name for Tenth Month.

9. Naitō Rosen (1654–1733) was the lord of Taira in Iwaki Province and a *haikai* poet.

10. Ki no Tsurayuki (884–946) was major Heian poet and author of Japan's first literary diary, *Tosa Diary* (*Tosa nikki*, 935). Chōmei was a court poet who later became a hermit, as described in his famous *Account of My Ten-foot Square Hut* (*Hōjōki*, 1212). In Bashō's time the anonymous *Account of a Journey to the Eastern Barrier* (*Tōkankikō*, 1242) was (inaccurately) attributed to him. The Nun Abutsu (d. 1283) was Kamakura poet and author of *Diary of the Waning Moon* (*Izayoi nikki*, 1279–80).

11. Huang Tingjian was a Chinese poet whose style was considered highly individualistic. Su Shi was a major Chinese poet and literary theorist who emphasized the value of freshness in poetry.

12. Bashō uses words adapted from chapter two of the *Zhuangzi* in which a character states that in order to understand his reckless words you must listen recklessly.

13. Asukai Masaaki (1611–79) was a *waka* poet and court noble in Kyōto.

14. Tsuboi Tokuku (d. 1690), Nagoya merchant and one of Bashō's favorite disciples.

15. Ochi Etsujin (1656–1739), a disciple of Bashō from Nagoya. He would accompany Bashō on the journey to Sarashina.

16. A game somewhat resembling chess, it is played with polished white and black stones.

17. The pun-filled waka might be translated: "From Kuwana I came / with nothing to eat; / morning passed at Hoshikawa / and after an endless day / I came to Hinaga" [*kuwana yori / kuwade kinureba / hoshikawa no / asake wa suginu / hinaga narikeri*].

18. Shunjōbō Shigemoto (1206–92) was the priest who is credited with reconstructing the famous Todaiji Temple in Nara.

19. It is said that two Sal trees withered and died when the Buddha passed into final nirvana.

20. Bashō alludes to the story of the priest Zōga, on pilgrimage to the Ise Shrine, who obeyed an order from a *kami* to give all his clothes to beggars.

21. Tokoku adopted the name "Ten Thousand Chrysanthemums Boy."

22. In a *haibun* that discusses this scene ("Preface to 'all the more I want to see it'"), Bashō reports: "It is said that the god here, Hitokotonushi-no-kami, has a hideous face, and people of the world have reviled him."

23. "Dragon's Gate" (*Ryūmon*) is the name of waterfall in Yoshino and also in China. The Chinese poet Li Bo was known for his love of waterfalls and wine.

24. Nijikō is an area of the Yoshino River known for powerful rapids. The mountain rose has yellow blossoms.

25. This sentence is preceded by the words "Seirei Falls." Apparently, Bashō intended to include a *hokku* after this name, but it does not appear in the text.

26. The *hokku* alludes to a *waka* attributed to Saigyō (see note 10).

27. Bashō alludes to a poem on Yoshino by Fujiwara Yoshitsune (1169–1206): "Long ago / who was it that / planted these cherry seeds, / making Yoshino / the mountain of blossoms?" [*mukashi tare / kakaru sakura no / tane o uete / yoshino o hana no / yama to nashikemu*].

28. Bashō refers to a *waka* by Saigyō: "Yoshino mountains: / departing from last year's / broken-branch path, / I will seek blossoms / along ways yet unseen" [*yoshino yama / kozo no shiori no / michi kaete / mada minukata no / hana o tazunen*].

29. Teishitsu, an early *haikai* poet of the Teitoku School, once was asked what words he had composed at Yoshino, and responded: "this! this! / my only words for blossoms / at Yoshino Mountain" [*kore wa kore wa / to bakari hana no / yoshino yama*].

30. Mount Kōya contains the mausoleum of Kūkai (774–835), founder of Shingon Buddhism in Japan, and a sophisticated religious thinker, popular spiritual leader, famous pilgrim, and poet of Chinese verse. Near his mausoleum are the remains of thousands of others, including Bashō's ancestors.

31. The topknot of hair signifies that he is a layman, rather than the more spiritually serious (and bald-headed) monk.

32. A scenic bay south of Osaka, famous in Japanese literature since early times because it literally means "Poetry Bay."

33. This sentence is preceded by the words "Kimii Temple," which appears to be a headnote for a *hokku*, but the poem is missing. It might refer to the previous *hokku*, since the temple is located on Waka Bay.

34. The *Tales of Saigyō* (*Saigyō monogatari*, date and author unknown) relates a story in which the poet is beaten and then dumped overboard from a crowded ferry. Saigyō accepted the situation with equanimity.

35. *Essays in Idleness* (*Tsurezuregusa*, 1330–32, by Yoshida Kenkō, 1274–1338), includes the story of the monk Shōkū who is pushed into a ditch when he encounters a lady on horseback along a narrow road. He becomes infuriated and shouts invectives, then is embarrassed by his anger and flees.

36. The first day of the Fourth Month was traditionally a day to change one's apparel to conform to the beginning of summer. On this journey Bashō lacks true summer clothes, so he simply removes one layer to fit the occasion, while Mangikumaru wants to get rid of his heavy coat.

37. A monk who founded the *Vinaya* school (*Ritsushū*) in Japan, one of the early six schools of Buddhism in the Nara period. The sect established regulations for clergy and rituals such as ordination that were approved by the Japanese

court. Ganjin departed for Japan in 742, but did not arrive until 754.

38. Bashō refers to a poem by Yukihira written during his exile in Suma: "If by chance / someone asks about me / tell them I live in loneliness / by Suma Bay, weeping / as I gather seaweed" [*wakuraba ni / tou hito araba / suma no ura ni / moshiotaretsutsu / wabu to kotae yo*].

39. A sillaginoid (*Sillago sihama*).

40. The battle of Ichi-no-tani (1184) was fought nearby, in which Yoshitsune led the Minamoto forces in a surprise attack that devastated the Heike army.

41. As related in *The Tales of the Heike*, Yoshitsune was led over the mountains to Ichi-no-tani by an eighteen- (rather than sixteen-) year-old guide.

42. Drawn from a line in the *Tale of Genji*, which is repeated in the Nō play *Wind in the Pines (Matsukaze)*.

43. In a poem "Climbing Yo-yang Tower," the Chinese poet Du Fu relates his view of these two regions.

44. Literally "Pine Wind" and "Spring Rain," they were sisters who were loved by Ariwara Yukihira during his exile in Suma. Their story is told in the famous Nō play *Wind in the Pines*.

45. When Yoshitsune attacked the Heike, the infant Emperor Antoku (r. 1180–85) and his family were routed. Bashō draws on the famous description of the battle in the *Tales of the Heike*.

CHAPTER 4. SARASHINA JOURNAL

1. Literally "abandon mountain," this place is famous for the legend, first recorded in *Tales of Yamato (Yamato monogatari*, 951?), of a village that would carry its elderly women to the mountains and leave them there to die. Eventually one son decided this act was unfilial and returned to the mountain to rescue his mother.

2. Yamamoto Kakei (1648–1716) was a poet and physician from Nagoya.

3. In Japanese the place names are Kakehashi, Nezame, Saru-ga-baba, and Tachitōge.

4. From a Buddhist poem that states that compared to our uncertain, transient world, the whirlpool at Awa seems free of wind and waves.

5. A Chinese-style verse by Ono Takamura (802–52) states that we should take the word "sorrow" and write it as "the heart of autumn."

6. Bashō uses obscure and even nonexistent characters here to suggest rare and precious objects.

7. In ancient times, horses from the various parts of Japan were presented to the court in mid-Eighth Month (about the time this *hokku* was written). A court envoy would meet the horses at this bridge.

CHAPTER 5.
THE NARROW ROAD TO THE DEEP NORTH

1. Alluding to preface to the poem "Giving a Banquet on a Spring Night in the Peach and Pear Garden" by the Chinese Tang poet Li Bo in which he says: "Heaven and earth are the inn for the ten thousand things, light and shadow are wayfarers of a hundred generations. And so this floating life is like a dream."

2. Guardin deity of the road.

3. Sugiyama Sanpū (1647–1732) was a disciple and wealthy patron of Bashō's.

4. 3rd day of Third Month is the Doll Festival (also Girl's Day or Peach Festival), in which dolls are displayed in houses. Bashō gave his hut to a family with girls.

5. First section and front page of a *renga* sequence.

6. The traditional name for Third Month, suggesting the "increasing life" (its literal meaning) of spring.

7. A Chinese metaphor for a distant, snowy country, which is found in Chinese poetry, Nō plays, etc. For example, from the Nō play *Snow on Bamboo*: "Though I've never been to the mountains of Wu, the weight of snow on my bamboo

hat, is it not the white hair of old age?" and in *A Zen Forest of Sayings* is the phrase, "my bamboo hat heavy with snow from Wu skies."

8. "Doorless furnace," a Shinto shrine, now Ōmiwa Shrine in the city of Tochigi.

9. The Sengen Shrine, in Fujinomiya City, Shizuoka.

10. The deity, Konohana Sakuyahime, was consort to Ninigi no Mikoto. When she proclaimed her pregnancy after one night with him, he doubted he was the father. To prove her children were divine, she walled herself into a building, set fire to it, and gave birth to three gods, one of which was Hohonodemi no Mikoto.

11. Although it was not included in *Narrow Road*, Bashō wrote the *hokku* "with threads of / heat waves it is interwoven: / the smoke" while he was Muro no Yashima.

12. A herring, *Chatoessus punctatus*. It is said that when cooked the fish smells like burnt flesh, the probable source of the prohibition.

13. Site of the mausoleum of Tokugawa Ieyasu (1542–1616), founder of the Tokugawa shogunate.

14. Literally "devoid of wisdom and discrimination." Scholars differ on whether this is criticism or praise. I take it positively as lacking artificiality, which parallels the other terms used. Note that the portrait begins with references to Buddhism and ends with references to Confucianism.

15. From the *Analects* of Confucius.

16. "Uzuki," Fourth Month (first month of summer), literally "month of the Deutzia flower."

17. According to a legend, the mountain was devastated by storms twice a year.

18. Farmer, warrior, artisan, and merchant were the four classes of Japanese feudalism. Compared with the bloody civil wars of the medieval period, Japan enjoyed relative peace and prosperity under the authoritarian shogunate of that time.

19. It was a custom to change to lighter weight clothes on the first day of summer (1st of Fourth Month), but in this case

Sora makes a more fundamental change to the robes of Buddhist monk and a more serious religious life.

20. *Musa bajoo*, the banana (or plantain) tree. A banana tree was planted by the hut built for him in Fukagawa, and Bashō used it for his pen name. The plant was traditionally associated with impermanence, and Bashō prized it also for its vulnerability to the elements (it tears easily) and its uselessness (it does not bear fruit in central Japan). See the *haibun*, "Words on Transplanting the *Bashō* Tree."

21. Matsushima and Kisagata are sites on his journey that are on the opposite coasts of Japan, thus a metonymy for all the sites of the trip.

22. It is traditional in Buddhism to undergo intensive practice at one's temple during the summer.

23. Kasane means "multi-layered." *Yae*, "eight-fold," is the term is used for double-petal flowers, while *nadeshiko* is the term for wild pinks, a flower associated with girls. There is no "double-petal pink" plant.

24. Jōbōji Takakatsu had pen names Tōsetsu and Shūa. His house is the subject of the *haibun* "Concerning the Beautiful Scenery at the Home of Master Shūa."

25. In the Kamakura period there was sport of shooting dogs with blunted arrows while riding on horseback.

26. Legend says that she was a fox spirit. See note 32, chapter 5.

27. Nasu no Yoichi was samurai who gained fame for shooting a fan hanging from a boat in the Battle of Yashima in 1185.

28. Named in honor of En no Gyōja (fl. 8th c.), founder of the mountain ascetic sect of Shugendō.

29. En no Gyōja's clogs were said to be unusually high and intentionally difficult to walk on, and Bashō's prayer to them was for strength and fortitude on his journey as he departed for the Deep North.

30. A Rinzai Zen monk (1643?–1715) from whom Bashō received spiritual training around 1682. Bashō visited Butchō during his journey to Kashima.

31. Japan adopted a Chinese custom of specifying a set of beautiful views in an area, in this case peaks, buildings, trees, rocks, and so forth, around the temple.

32. The Chinese monk Yuanmiao is said to have practiced Zen for fifteen years in a cave he called "Barrier of Death," while the monk Fayun discoursed on Buddhism all day long in a lean-to huddled among boulders.

33. Located near the hot springs in Nasu, the Killing Stone is a boulder (about seven feet square and four feet high), around which noxious gases rise. A legend assigns the origin of the stone to a fox spirit that transformed itself into a beautiful woman, Lady Tamamo. She succeeded in becoming the favorite mistress of Emperor Toba (1103–56), but was exposed by an exorcist. The fox then fled to the Nasu Plain, where it was killed, its vengeful spirit taking the form of the stone. Bashō wrote the following *hokku* there: "the stench of the stone— / the summer grass red, / the scorching dew" [*ishi no ka ya / natsugusa akaku / tsuyu atsushi*].

34. The passage draws on a waka by Saigyō: "By the roadside / a crystal stream flowing / in the shade of a willow: / 'Just a moment,' I thought— / yet I've lingered long" [*michinobe ni / shimizu nagaruru / yanagi kage / shibashi tote koso / tachidomaritsure*]. The Nō play *The Wandering Priest and the Willow* was based on Saigyō's verse.

35. Refers to a *waka* by Taira no Kanemori (d. 990): "Were there some way, / somehow, I'd send word / to those in the capital: / today I have crossed / the Shirakawa Barrier" [*tayori araba / ikade miyako e / tsugeyaran / kyō shirakawa no / seki wa koen to*].

36. The other two are the Nakoso Barrier in Hitachi and the Nezu Barrier in Dewa.

37. Refers to a poem by Priest Nōin (d. 998): "I left the capital / along with the spring haze, / but now the autumn wind / is blowing across / the Shirakawa Barrier" (*miyako o ba / kasumi to tomoni / tachishikado / akikaze zo fuku / shirakawa no seki*). Nōin was a famous Heian monk-poet who traveled in the north country.

38. Refers to a *waka* by Minamoto Yorimasa (1104–80): "In the capital / I beheld leaves / still green, but now / crimson leaves lie all around / at the Shirakawa Barrier" [*miyako*

niwa / mada aoba nite / mishika domo / momiji chiri-shiku / shirakawa no seki].

39. Fujiwara no Kiyosuke (1104–77) recorded this story in his collection of poetics and anecdotes, *Fukuro no sōshi.*

40. Sagara Izaemon (1638–1715), a high official at Sukagawa Station.

41. The word translated as "all art" is *fūryū,* an extraordinarily complex term, including associations of high culture, art in general, poetry, and music, as well as ascetic wayfaring and Daoist eccentricity. Bashō sees the roots of these various qualities, including high art, in rural culture. See Peipei Qiu's studies of this term in *Adaptation and Transformation* (Honolulu: University of Hawaii Press, forthcoming).

42. Draws on a *waka* by Saigyō: "Deep in the mountains, / I'll collect water / dripping from the rocks / while picking up horse chestnuts / that plop down from time to time" [*yama fukami / iwa ni shitadaru / mizu tomen / katsugatsu otsuru / tochi hirou hodo*]. The floating world refers to the common life of pleasure and pain, especially in the city. See also the *hokku* "chestnuts of Kiso: / for those of the floating world, / my souvenir" in *Sarashina Journal.*

43. This chestnut (*Castanea crenata*) is found in out-of-the-way places and has inconspicuous blossoms.

44. A Buddhist monk (668–749) who once was arrested for preaching to the masses and developing social welfare programs, but later was made archbishop and helped with fundraising for the building of Tōdaiji Temple.

45. Probably a species of blue flag iris, mentioned in *waka* poetry. However, the identity of the plant remained uncertain in Bashō's time, and still is disputed today.

46. *Shinobu* is a complex term: it is the name of the region famous in poetry that he is visiting, it is two verbs meaning "to endure" and "to recall longingly," and it is used in the name of the hare's-foot fern *shinobugusa* (grass of longing remembrance).

47. A local custom of dyeing clothes by using the patterns on a large stone. This practice was made famous in a poem in the early poetry collection *Kokinshū* (905–920).

48. The wives of two brothers, Satō Tsugunobu and Satō Tadanobu, who died fighting for Yoshitsune. When they died, the wives are said to have worn their husband's armor to console their mother.

49. Yanghu, a governor in China, was so loved that when he died, people could not help weeping whenever they viewed his gravestone, which became known as the Gravestone of Weeping.

50. Minamoto Yoshitsune (1159–89) was a great general in the war against the Heike, but after victory his older brother Yoritomo had him hunted down. Benkei (d. 1189) was a warrior monk and Yoshitsune's chief retainer, who died trying to defend him. Both became legends celebrated in various genres of Japanese literature.

51. There are various theories about his illness, with gallstones one possibility.

52. Fujiwara Sanekata (d. 998), was a Heian poet who was exiled to the north country. Failing to dismount as he rode past a shrine at Kasashima, he was immediately killed when he fell from his horse.

53. Saigyō visited Sanetaka's grave and wrote: "Never to decay: / only the name / he left behind; / I gaze at his memento, / a miscanthus in a withered field" [*kuchimosenu / sono na bakari o / todomeokite / kareno no susuki / katami nizo miru*].

54. Written about in classical poetry and replanted several times.

55. When Nōin visited here a second time, there was no pine to be found, and he wrote: "Pine of Takekuma: / at this time / there is no trace of it, / have a thousand years passed / since I last came?" [*takekuma no / matsu wa kono tabi / ato mo nashi / chitose o hete ya / ware wa kitsuran*].

56. Bashō saw the cherries bloom in Edo, and now he has arrived at the famous Takekuma Pine. The word *miki* means "saw," "trunks," and "three trees." *Matsu* means both "pine" and "wait for."

57. The 5th day of Fifth Month is the Boy's Festival, also called Iris Festival because people hang irises from the roofs.

People were preparing for the event on the 4th day, when Bashō arrived.

58. The bush clover is *Lespedeza bicolor*, a shrub with purple blossoms in early autumn. Pieris is *Pieris japonica*, a white blossoming shrub in the Rhododendron family. These areas became known by a poem by Minamoto Toshiyori: "Seize and tether them, / the horses loose at / Tamada and Yokono: / on Azalea Hill, / the pieris are in bloom" [*toritsunage / tamada yokono no / hanare uma / tsutsuji no oka ni / asemi sakunari*].

59. From an anonymous waka in the *Kokinshū*: "Attendants, / tell your lord, / 'Sir, the umbrella': / in the Miyagi Fields the dew under the trees / is worse than rain" [*misaburai / mikasa to mōse / miyagino no / ki no no shita tsuyu wa / ame ni masareri*].

60. Yakushi is the Buddha of Healing. Tenjin refers to Sugawara Michizane (845–903), who became the deity of learning after he died.

61. The two generals from the Nara period (710–84) had the role of securing the "pacification" of the "northern barbarians."

62. Reigned 724–49, the forty-fifth emperor.

63. Offshore rock and Sue no Matsuyama are scenes famous in classical poetry. Masshōzan is Sue no Matsuyama (Last Pine Mountain) read in Sino-Japanese.

64. Images of eternal love in the Chinese poet Bo Juyi's famous narrative poem, "Song of Everlasting Regret."

65. Refers to an anonymous poem in the *Kokinshū*: "Michinoku: / every place is alluring, / but at Shiogama / there is such sadness / as rowboats are pulled to shore" [*michinoku wa / izuku wa aredo / shiogama no / ura kogu fune no / tsunade kanashi mo*].

66. The *Tales of the Heike* were often performed with music of the *biwa* (a stringed instrument), and ballad dances (*kōwakamai*) performed the feats of heroes.

67. Date Masamune (1565–1636), patron of the arts.

68. The year was 1187. Izumi Saburō was Fujiwara Tadahira (1167–89), who died at the hands of his brother while defending Yoshitsune.

69. From the Chinese philosopher Han Yu.

70. One of the most famous scenic places in Japan, made of many small islands.

71. Two lakes in China famous for their beauty.

72. A river in China with exceptionally strong tides at its narrow estuary.

73. God of the Mountains.

74. *Zōka*, an important term in Bashō's cosmology, derived from Chinese philosophy and aesthetics. See note 7, chapter 3.

75. A monk from Myōshin Temple in Kyōto who lived 1582–1659. In 1636 he rebuilt Zuigan Temple in Matsushima.

76. Yamaguchi Sodō (1642–1716), a *haikai* and Chinese verse poet, and Hara Anteki (dates unknown), a *waka* poet and physician in Edo.

77. Or Dakushi, dates unknown.

78. A thirteenth-century monk, who actually visited Song rather than Tang China. Bashō makes several mistakes in historical detail in this section.

79. A twelfth-century monk admired by Saigyō. He is said to have confined himself for twelve years in a temple in Ojima to recite the *Lotus Sutra*. He appears in tale seventeen of the *Senjushō*.

80. This passage is dotted with the names of places famous in Japanese culture (*utamakura*). For translations of poems related to each one, see Hiroaki Sato, *Bashō's Narrow Road* (Berkeley: Stone Bridge, 1996), 82–84.

81. In 749 it was announced that gold was discovered in a mountain in Michinoku. Ōtomo no Yakamochi (718–85) made a set of poems celebrating this, concluding with an envoy that proclaimed that gold had bloomed.

82. Fujiwara no Kiyohira (1056–1128), Motohira (dates unknown), and Hidehira (d. 1187), established a powerful

court at Hiraizumi. It was destroyed in the following generation by Minamoto Yoritomo, who involved Hidehira's sons on opposite sides of the struggle with Yoritomo's brother Yoshitsune. Both sons were killed and the court annihilated.

83. Famous lines from Du Fu's poem "A Spring View," written after the disastrous An Lushan Rebellion of 735.

84. Masuo Kanefusa, loyal retainer to Yoshitsune, who in old age died fighting at Hiraizumi.

85. Amida Buddha and his attendants Kannon and Seishi.

86. Literally, "peeing in front," which Bashō draws on in the *hokku*.

87. Drawn from a line in a poem by Du Fu: "As I climb the windy stone steps, a dust storm blows from the edge of the clouds."

88. Suzuki Seifū, 1651–1721, a wealthy safflower merchant and prominent *haikai* poet in Obanazawa.

89. 794–864, Tendai Buddhist also known as Ennin. He also founded Zuigan Temple mentioned earlier.

90. Considered one of the three swiftest rivers in Japan.

91. The earlier schools of Danrin and Teimon, as opposed to Bashō's newer Shōmon school.

92. *Rokaku* (reed flute) is a neologism that suggests this region's rustic culture, which nonetheless had profound aesthetic effects.

93. Bashō uses the word *michi* (way or path) three times in this part of the sentence.

94. The ambiguity of this last line had led to diverse interpretations and translations. I attempt to keep some of that ambiguity, as well as both of Bashō's use of "this" (*kono*).

95. *Goten* was a rock formation that is said to resemble the stones used in the game of Go, and the *Hayabusa* rapids literally means "falcon."

96. Refers to an anonymous poem in the *Kokinshū* that mentions riceboats on the Mogami River.

97. Bashō alludes to a line from Bo Juyi: "A fragrant wind comes from the south." Bashō also may have in mind a

Chinese poem attributed to Su Shi: "Everyone suffers from the heat / But I love this long day of summer. / Coming from the south a delightful breeze / makes the palace cool."

98. *Engi shiki* is a fifty-volume collection of laws, rituals, prayers, and so forth, compiled in 927. Actually there is no mention of Satoyama in the text. The *Fudoki* are eighth-century "topographies," physical and cultural geographies of various provinces compiled by imperial decree. Few survive.

99. The Chinese character for *kuro* ("black") consists of two sections which, if misread, could be taken for the two characters *sato* (village) and *yama* (mountain). *Ushū* is the sinified reading for the province of Dewa, with *u* meaning "feather," and if the character *shū* is dropped, the three characters spell "feather black mountain" (*haguroyama*).

100. The three principal mountains of Dewa Province. Mount Haguro, "Black Feather Mountain," is the headquarters of the Haguro sect of *Shugendō* and rises to about 1,300 feet high. Gassan, "Mount Moon," is around 6,000 feet, and Yudono, "Bath Hall," is around 4,500 feet.

101. Paper cords and turbans were special accoutrements for those entering the holy precincts. Cords made of paper were worn around the neck, and white cloth was wrapped around the head.

102. A swordsmith believed to have lived in the twelfth century with the name of Gassan.

103. A spring in Zhejiang Province in China was famous as a place for crafting swords.

104. Husband and wife in ancient China who were famous swordsmiths.

105. A Tendai monk (d. 1135) who wrote: "Together, / let us feel the pathos, / mountain cherry: / other than your blossoms / there is no one here I know" [*morotomo ni / aware to omoe / yamakazura / hana yori hoka ni / shiru hito mo nashi*].

106. Bashō's phrase is elusive, leading to various interpretations and translations. I have tried to retain the rich ambiguity.

107. Anyone entering this ascetic center had to relinquish all the money he was carrying, so that pilgrims entered walking on a path of coins.

108. Shigeyuki and Fugyoku were poets in Bashō's school. Shigeyuki's dates are unknown, and Fugyoku died in 1697.

109. Here as many other places, Bashō plays with the literal meaning of place names. *Atsumi* means "hot," *Fuku* means "blow" (and thus suggests coolness.)

110. A volcano, 4,900 feet high, about thirteen miles southeast of Kisagata.

111. Draws on a line from a verse by Su Shi: "when misty rain obscures the mountain, the view is stirring also." In that poem, he compares the loveliness of the West Lake to that of the famous Lady Xi Shi, who was said to be beautiful in every situation.

112. "The cherry trees / of Kisagata are buried / under the waves, / as fisherman row their boats, / over waves of blossoms" [*kisagata no / sakura wa nami ni / uzumorete / hana no ue kogu / ama no tsuribune*]. The poem is no longer considered to be by Saigyō.

113. Empress Jingū is said to have ruled in Japan in the third century, but details of her activities are very uncertain.

114. *Nebu*, a small tree (*Albizzia julibrissin*) with feathery compound leaves and pink blossoms in summer. *Nebu* is also read as *nemu*, which means "to sleep."

115. These shutters could be removed and placed on the ground as a seat.

116. A vow of unbroken fidelity, with which ospreys were traditionally associated.

117. Actually, it took Bashō sixteen days to make it to Ichiburi Barrier from Sakata.

118. Sixth night refers to the Tanabata star festival of the seventh night of Seventh Month, the one time of the year that the Weaver Girl (the star Vega) and the Herd Boy (Altair) meet. On that night, magpies form a bridge of wings across the River of Heaven (the Milky Way), which allows the Herd Boy to cross.

119. An island in the Sea of Japan, where several famous people were exiled.

120. Oyashirazu, Koshirazu, Inumodori, Komagaeshi: Treacherous places by a coastal cliff where the surf could engulf the road.

121. Draws on an anonymous *waka:* "If I were a / daughter of the shore / who lived out her life on the beach / where the white waves break, / my dwelling too would be uncertain" [*shiranami no / yosuru nagisa ni / yo o sugusu / ama no ko nareba / yado mo sadamezu*]. "Daughter of the shore" refers to a seaside prostitute.

122. This entire passage has given rise to voluminous and varied commentary, and should be compared to the abandoned baby passage near the beginning of *Journal of Bleached Bones in a Field.* For one interpretation, see my "Impermanence, Fate, and the Journey: Bashō and the Problem of Meaning," *Religion* 16 (1986): 323–341.

123. River that washes into the Sea of Japan in Toyama Bay, Etchū Province.

124. An image used in several poems about Tako Bay in the *Man'yōshū.*

125. Ariso-umi, the sea around Fushiki Harbor.

126. Mount Deutzia Blossoms, *U-no-hana-yama*, was sung about in the *Man'yōshū*, and Kurikara Valley was the site of a 1183 battle in which Kiso no Yoshinaka (1154–84) defeated forces of the Taira clan.

127. Kasho (d. 1731), from Osaka (Ōzaka), and Kosugi Isshō (1653–1688) were followers of Bashō's school.

128. Komatsu, on the Sea of Japan in Kaga Province.

129. Saitō Sanemori (1111–83) was seventy-three years old when he dyed his hair black to hide his age in the Battle of Shinohara. Originally he was in service to the Minamoto clan, but he was killed at Shinohara fighting for the rival Taira clan. The story is presented in the *Tales of the Heike* and the Nō play, *Sanemori.*

130. Minamoto Yoshitomo (1147–99), father of politically successful Yoritomo and the tragic hero Yoshitsune.

131. Kiso Yoshinaka (1154–84), a Minamoto military leader.

132. Dates unknown, a friend of Sanemori.
133. Emperor Kazan lived 968 to 1008. He reigned 984–86 and then was forced to abdicate at eighteen years old, after which he made an extensive pilgrimage.
134. Kannon (Avalokitesvara in Sanskrit), the Bodhisattva of compassion "who hears the cries of the world."
139. The first and last of the Thirty Three Temples visited by Kazan: Seigando-ji and Kegon-ji.
136. *Ishiyama* literally means "stone mountain." Bashō may see the stones at Nata Temple (built on a hill of whitish quartz trachyte) as whiter than the famous white stones of Stone Mountain near Lake Biwa in Ōmi Province, or he may experience the wind as whiter than the stones. In traditional East Asia, autumn was associated with white.
137. Probably the Arima hot springs.
138. Chrysanthemums (and their fragrance and dew on the blossoms) were traditionally associated in East Asia with health and longetivity.
139. Izumiya Jinzaemon (1676–1751), who was fourteen years old at that time.
140. Yasuhara Masaaki (1610–73) and Matsunaga Teitoku (1571–1653), the founder of the Teimon School.
141. A lapwing bird is about the size of a pigeon but with longer legs. Like the mandarin duck, it is associated with fidelity. The image is drawn from Chinese poetry.
142. It was customary for travelers to write a phrase on their hats concerning their companions, which Bashō now erases as Sora leaves him. Dew was a traditional image for tears as well as impermanence.
143. A traditional idea in Chinese literature. A league (Japanese, *ri*) is approximately 2.4 miles.
144. It was customary for a traveling monk who spent the night at a temple to sweep the garden before he left.
145. Shiogoshi, on the Japan Sea, famous for its pine trees.
146. Bashō follows the traditional attribution of this poem to Saigyō, which is disputed by modern scholars.

147. Bashō alludes to the opening passage to chapter eight of the *Zhuangzi*, where the author compares Confucian morality to unnatural and useless appendages.

148. As weather cools in early autumn, the fan used for summer heat is discarded. Bashō had written something on it, however, making it difficult to part with.

149. While most aspiring Buddhist leaders in early Japan sought to establish prominence in or near the capital, Dōgen (1200–1253), the founder of Sōtō Zen, deliberately built his temple in remote mountains.

150. Kanbe Tōsai (dates uncertain), a poet of the Teitoku school in Fukui.

151. Moonflower, *yūgao* (evening face), is a vine that resembles the morning glory. Snake gourd, *hechima*, is a vine that blooms yellow in summer and produces gourds in autumn. Cockscomb, *keitō*, is an annual that blooms red, yellow, or white in late summer and fall, and its leaves turn red in autumn. Goosefoot, *hahakigi* (broom tree), is an annual that blooms pale green in late summer and fall. *Hahakigi* is the name of a chapter in *The Tale of Genji*.

152. The scene echoes the *Yūgao* chapter of *The Tale of Genji*, in which Genji muses that he feels as if he were in a tale of long ago.

153. The fourteenth emperor and husband of Empress Jingū, said to have ruled 192–200.

154. *Yugyō*, the title of each patriarch of the Ji sect of Buddhism. The second was Taa Shōnin (1237–1319), who succeeded the founder, Ippen Shōnin (1239–89).

155. *Iro no hama*, which derives its name from the pink masuo shells.

156. Ten'ya Gorōzaemon (dates unknown) was a shipper and *haikai* poet in Tsuruga.

157. Hokke means Lotus Blossom, signifying the Lotus Sutra and thus, the Nichiren sect of Buddhism.

158. Famous as a place of exile, which links it with melancholy and autumn.

159. Futami, literally "two views," is the area around the Great Shrine at Ise, known for clams and for the Wedded Rocks

(two boulders in the sea tied together with a huge rope). *Futa* also means a lid (in this case, of a clam), while *mi* can mean both "see" and "flesh"; *futa mi ni wakareru* means to divide the clam meat from the shell. The second hokku of this journal, in which Bashō leaves for the Deep North, begins "departing spring."

CHAPTER 6. SAGA DIARY

1. *Honchō ichinin isshū*, ed. by Hayashi Shunsai (1618–80).
2. *Yotsugi monogatari*, which may refer to *Tales of Flowering Fortunes (Eiga monogatari*, 1028–37) or *The Great Mirror (Okagami*, 1119).
3. See note 10, chapter 3.
4. *Shōyō meisho wakashū*, edited by the poet Sokei in 1660, a collection of *waka* about celebrated sites in Japan, organized by the order of Japanese syllabary.
5. Noon. The hour of the horse was 11:00 A.M. to 1:00 P.M.
6. A bodhisattva venerated in Shingon Buddhism, especially by Kūkai.
7. As told in the *Tales of the Heike*, Kogō no Tsubone was once the favorite of Emperor Takakura (1161–81), but was forced out of the court, finding refuge in Saga. The Emperor's minister Nakakuni found her from the sound of her koto, and she was brought back to court. Later she was forced out again and became a nun. Subsequently the Emperor fell ill and died, and Kogō drowned herself in the Ōi River.
8. Bashō refers to a poem by Bo Juyi: "The blossoms at the shrine of the goddess of Wu are more crimson than her lipstick. / The willows of Wang Zhao-jun village are more green than her mascara."
9. Disciple of Bashō and wife of Bonchō.
10. The *yu* (or *yuzu*) tree, which resembles the lemon or lime, is *Citrus junos* of the Rue family.
11. Bashō, his disciples Mukai Kyorai (1651–1704), Nozawa Bonchō (d. 1714), and Ukō, and probably a servant who carried the food.

12. Bashō from Iga Province, Bonchō from Kaga, Kyorai from Hizen, and Josō from Owari.

13. Saigyō's poem is: "No longer hoping / for any visitors: / in this mountain village / were there no loneliness, / dwelling here would be misery" [*tou hito mo / omoitaetaru / yamazato no / sabishisa nakuba / sumiukaramashi*].

14. The bird Bashō refers to is the Common Cuckoo (*kankodori* or *kakkō: Cuculus canorus*), but he uses an alternative name that literally means "little calling bird." He slightly misquotes Saigyō's original text (*yamazato ni / tare o mata kowa / yobukodori / hitori nomi koso / sumamu to omou ni*), but the meaning of Bashō's version is virtually the same.

15. Kinoshita Chōchōshi (1569–1649) became a monk and *waka* poet after he lost his land holdings in political maneuverings following the foundation of the Tokugawa Shogunate.

16. At the Daichiin Temple in Nagashima, Ise Province.

17. Kawai Otokuni (dates unknown) became a disciple of Bashō during the *Narrow Road to the Deep North* journey. A rich merchant in Ōtsu, he provided Bashō with financial support.

18. Sōha is a Zen monk and poet who lived in Edo near the Bashō Hut. He traveled to Kashima with Bashō.

19. The length of two bows is about fifteen feet.

20. Osmund and bracken ferns were used as edible plants in spring, with brackens preferred and appearing earlier. Brackens had the poetic epithet of "purple dusted," so the royal fern was dust among dust.

21. Isoda Shōbō (dates unknown).

22. Mikami Senna (1651–1723), Bashō's disciple.

23. The red fruit of the persimmon.

24. The summer cuckoo sings as it flies near the Japanese Hackberry (*Celtis sinensis* var. *japonica*), recalling spring birds around the plum and cherry.

25. A Chinese Song Dynasty poet.

26. A volume of linked verse that is completed in the time it takes a candle to burn five *bu* (approximately one inch).

27. In the *renga* tradition, a stanza is appreciated, not as an independent verse, but in the way it links to the previous stanza. As a result, two stanzas are sometimes presented, with the only author of the second link identified.

28. *Hanzoku* literally means "half monk" and thus half-lay person. Priestly attire included a medicine box, usually carried on the hip.

29. The typhoon winds ruin the shack used by the fisherman, who gives it to a criminal exiled in the area.

30. Or Abstinence Day, a Buddhist day of spiritual purification.

31. After the hour of the monkey is 4:00 to 5:00 P.M.

32. A *momme* is about 3.5 grams.

33. Thunder.

34. A deciduous shrub (*Deutzia scabra* or *D. crenata*) with tiny white blossoms in early summer.

35. A mail carrier regularly delivered mail between Edo and Kyōto, usually delivered every ten days.

36. Bashō visited this area during his journey to the Deep North.

37. Kōno Riyū (1662–1705) was chief priest at Meishō Temple and one of Bashō's disciples. Hirata is in the modern city of Hikone. Goshū is the Chinese-style name for Omi Province.

38. It was customary for the bridegroom, accompanied by his wife, to bring rice-cakes to her parents on the first Boy's Day (5th day of Fifth Month) after the wedding. The *hokku* is preceded by a headnote the meaning of which is unknown.

SELECTED *HAIBUN*

1. The Chinese poet Bo Juyi.

2. Bashō refers to a poem by Ariwara Yukihira (818–93) written during his exile in Suma, the last line of which is literally "respond that I live in *wabi*": "If by chance / someone

asks about me / tell them I live in loneliness / by Suma Bay,
weeping / as I gather seaweed" [*wakuraba ni / tou hito
araba / suma no ura ni / moshiotaretsutsu / wabu to kotae
yo*].

3. The Chinese poet Du Fu was called the "Elder Du," while
   Du Mu was called the "Younger Du."
4. The poem is "My Thatched Roof is Torn by the Autumn
   Wind."
5. *Wabi*, a term that he used frequently in his *haibun* of this
   period, includes notions of austerity, loneliness, and aesthetic beauty.
6. From a poem by Du Fu.
7. One of Bashō's pen names.
8. Draws on the famous poem by Priest Mansei: "To what
   shall I / compare this world? / The white wake / of a boat
   heading off / at daybreak" [*yo no naka o / nani ni tatoemu
   / asaborake / kogiyuku fune no / ato no shiranami*].
9. Draws from a poem by Saigyō: "That spring in Naniwa / in
   the land of Tsu: / was it but a dream? / The wind whipping
   through / the withered reeds" [*tsu no kuni no / naniwa no
   haru wa / yume nare ya / ashi no kareba ni / kaze wataruru
   nari*].
10. The three words mean past, present, and future
11. "Empty Chestnuts" is a linked-verse collection, edited by
    Takarai Kikaku (1661–1707) in 1683.
12. Two famous Chinese poets of the Tang period. They are
    often thought of as complementary pairs, with Li Bo seen
    as wild and exuberant and Du Fu more sober and socially
    concerned.
13. Literally "Cold Mountain," a poet of the Tang dynasty
    (dates uncertain). Han San has become somewhat of a Zen
    Buddhist legend, the epitome of the laughing hermit who
    lives an austere but carefree life in the mountains.
14. This phrase suggests a tie between these three poets' works
    and the Japanese aesthetic ideal of *yūgen* (mystery and
    depth), particularly the vague, indefinable, but moving
    quality associated with that term.

15. *Wabi* and *fūga*. See the glossary.

16. An allusion to a poem by Saigyō: "Deep in the mountains, / I'll collect water / dripping from the rocks / while picking up horse chestnuts / that plop down from time to time" [*yama fukami / iwa ni shitaru / mizu tomemu / katsukatsu otsuru / tochi hirou hodo*].

17. Xi Shi was an ancient Chinese beauty. Komurasaki was a contemporary courtesan of the Yoshiwara district of Edo famous for her beauty.

18. A reference to the ancient Chinese text *Book of History*: "The Yellow Emperor made a jeweled tripod kettle, patterned after the triad of Heaven, Earth, and Human." This image, of course, is meant as hyperbolic praise, but it also suggests that there is a connection between the creative process and cosmology.

19. By Matsuyama city in modern Ehime prefecture.

20. The phrase (*hito ni kokoro o tsuku*) alludes to a poem by Saigyō: "Even for one / who usually cares little / for things of the world / they stir the heart: / first winds of autumn" [*oshinabete / mono o omowanu / hito ni sae / kokoro o tsukuru / aki no hatsukaze*].

21. This and several other images in this *haibun* are drawn from the *Zhuangzi*, which discusses the artistic creativity and transformations of the universe.

22. A mythical range of mountains in the distant west where immortals dwell. It appears in the *Zhuangzi* and is referred to often in Chinese literature.

23. They are also fabled mountains associated with Daoist immortals (*Hōrai* and *Hōjō* in Japanese).

24. This refers to another mountain, mentioned in the first chapter of the *Zhuangzi*.

25. The word literally is "exhaust" (*tsukusu*), the same word translated as "exhaust" in the *haibun*. This term is an important one in Chinese aesthetic theory, with a range of meanings. Here the point seems to be that human art cannot exhaust the rich and shifting creativity of nature. Only nature can do so, in its own creative flux of every moment.

26. Bashō refers to the poem cited in note 4, introduction.

27. Chinese poet famous for his gentlemanly agrarian recluse life.

28. Said to be the home of the Chinese recluses Xu You and Cao Fu. The mountain is in the modern province of Henan.

29. The cotton-beating bow was used to make soft cotton yarn. It made a sound that resembled a lute.

30. In a popular story, Chikusai was a comical doctor who lost his patients because he kept indulging in "wild poetry." (*Kyō* means both crazy and comic.) Commentators disagree on whether "a wild poem" is a title or the first line of the *hokku*.

31. Kasyapa was the only disciple of the Buddha who smiled in realization when the Buddha gave his "flower sermon," in which he held up a flower and said nothing.

32. Several of the preceding images are drawn from chapter one of the *Zhuangzi*. Those who are content with little are praised, and the spiritual ideal is presented as sporting in the country of "Not-Even-Anything," to use Burton Watson's felicitous translation of this fantasyland in *Complete Works of Chuang Tzu* (New York: Columbia University Press, 1968).

33. Alludes to a verse by Saigyō: "Clouds appearing / now and then / covering its light / entertain the moon / and adorn its beauty" [*nakanaka ni / tokidoki kumo no / kakru koso / tsuki o motenasu / kazari narikere*].

34. The cup suggests moon (*tsuki*), and three suggests full (*mitsu*). Li Bo's poem is: "A bottle of wine under the blossoms, / drinking all alone. / Raising the cup to the bright moon, / with the shadow we become three." The image of a single moon reflected in multiple objects was a traditional symbol of unity-with-multiplicity characteristic of East Asian metaphysics.

35. The original poem by Bashō is "bagworms: / come hear their cry; / a thatched hut" [*minomushi no / ne o kiki ni koyo / kusa no io*]. Sodō wrote "Essay on the Bagworm" (1687) in response to it, then Chōko completed a painting

inspired by these works, and finally Bashō wrote his own essay reflecting back on the entire creative enterprise.

36. Bashō refers to a *waka* Saigyō wrote at Ise: "What divine being / graces this place / I know not and yet / feeling so deeply blessed / my tears spill forth" [*nanigoto no / owashimasu ka wa / shiranedomo / katajikenasa ni / namida koboruru*].

37. There is an allusion to lines from a poem by Bo Juyi: "A pile of gold after death / is not worth a cask of wine while alive."

38. *Thujopsis dolobrata*, false hiba cedar or hiba arborvitae. The *asunarō* looks like a hinoki cypress, a tree whose wood is highly prized while that of the false cypress is not. Literally, *asunarō* means "tomorrow I will become," and the context implies "tomorrow I will become a cypress." The *asunarō* seems to be what it is not; it appears to fall short of what one might expect it to achieve. This theme of incompletion is a complex and important one in Bashō's writings.

39. A Shingon Buddhist mountain community south of Kyōto. Bashō's family was associated with the Shingon sect.

40. Based on a waka by Gyōgi: The mountain pheasant / calls plaintively; / hearing its voice I wonder, / is that my father, / is that my mother? [*yamadori no / horohoro to naku / koe kikeba / chichi ka to zo omou / haha ka to zo omou*].

41. Bashō wanted to be at Obasute in Sarashina to see the harvest moon on the 15th day of Eighth Month.

42. From an account of the legend in *Tales of Yamato*, the waka later included in the *Kokinshū*: "My heart / cannot be consoled, / here at Sarashina: / gazing upon the moon / on Mount Obasute" [*waga kokoro / nagusamekanetsu / sarashina ya / obasuteyama ni / teru tsuki o mite*].

43. A famous mountain in China visited by numerous poets.

44. The 9th day of Ninth Month is the Chrysanthemum Festival, when the blossoms are supposedly at their peak. Like the 16th night for the moon, for the blossoms the 10th day of the month is one day past prime. In both cases, beauty remains, tinged now with the sadness of their fading.

45. In the Buddhist tradition, "withered" is a symbol of thorough realization.

46. These early medieval ballads were originally chanted by minstrels.

47. Etsujin accompanied Bashō on the 1687 journey that resulted in *Knapsack Notebook*, which included snow viewing on the Pacific coast.

48. *Yo* here can mean "world," "period," or "generation." 3rd day of Third Month was the "Doll's Festival," when dolls were displayed. This is the opening *hokku* in *Narrow Road to the Deep North*.

49. This episode is presented in slightly different form early in *The Narrow Road to the Deep North*, where the deputy of the local castle offers Bashō a horse and guide.

50. The scene of a monk on pilgrimage stopping at a place where he encounters something unusual is typical of Nō plays.

51. A town northwest of Kurobane in Shimotsuke Province during the *Narrow Road to the Deep North* journey. The name includes the word for "high."

52. Bashō used this epithet also at the beginning of *Knapsack Notebook*.

53. This is a *wakiku*, the second verse of a linked sequence. The cuckoo is notoriously difficult to glimpse.

54. The Iwase region is in Iwashiro Province.

55. Bashō's friend, Sagara Tōkyū, who lived 1638–1715.

56. Bashō is referring to the Shirakawa Barrier by alluding to the name of a barrier in China mentioned in a poem by Wang Wei.

57. On *fūryu*, see note 41 in chapter 5 and the glossary.

58. For *shinobu*, see note 46 in chapter 5.

59. The local custom of dyeing clothes with patterns from a large stone was made famous in poems in the *Kokinshū*.

60. See note 52, chapter 5.

61. Tsuruga is port city on the Sea of Japan in Echizen Province. Kei Shrine is the principle Shinto shrine in the area.

62. Each successor to Taa, the second Yugyō Shonin, ritually carries sand to the shrine.

63. Suma was well-known in classical literature for its desolate atmosphere in autumn, related to its use as a place of exile.

64. Akechi Mitsuhide (sixteenth century) fell into such poverty he could not afford to offer a *renga* party. His wife secretly cut and sold her hair so he could. He vowed that within fifty days he would rise to power and she would ride in a jeweled palanquin. He fulfilled his vow.

65. Bashō is referring to a verse by *renga* and early *haikai* poet Yamazaki Sōkan (fl. early sixteenth c.): "The best are those that don't come, / the next are those that never even sit down, / the lowest are those that stay. / Those that stay two nights / are the lowest of the low" [*jō wa kozu / chū wa kite inu / ge wa tomaru / niya tomaru wa / gege no ge no kyaku*].

66. Alludes to a poem by Su Shi.

67. Yuiitsu and Ryōbu are two versions of syncretism between Shinto and Buddhism. The Yuiitsu (one only) School of Shinto presented Shinto as the basis of Buddhism, Confucianism, and Daoism. The Ryōbu (dual) School gives a Shingon Buddhist version of Shinto, in which Shinto deities are equivalent to Buddhas.

68. Zeze Castle and Seta Bridge.

69. Mount Tanakami is famed for its shrines and graves related to celebrated poets.

70. Actually there is no such poem in this early collection of poetry.

71. As he did in *Journal of Bleached Bones in a Field* and *Knapsack Notebook*, Bashō refers to a *waka* attributed to Saigyō. See note 10, introduction.

72. A reference to an anecdote in the *Zhuangzi*, in which Penumbra and Shadow have a discussion. (See Burton Watson, trans. *The Complete Works of Chuang Tzu* (New York: Columbia University Press, 1968), p. 49.) An example of Bashō's complex nondualism, here associated particularly with Daoism. The dichotomy is not limited to moral right and wrong but includes all dualities and judgments.

73. Another instance of Bashō's nondualism as well as the important theme of dream and unreality in his work.

74. Bashō refers to his own *hokku:* "sunk in sorrow, / make me feel loneliness: / mountain cuckoo" [*uki ware o / sabishigarase yo / kankodori*].

75. Unchiku lived 1632–1703.

76. Ono no Komachi, famous Heian poet, who traditionally has been portrayed as going from beautiful young lover to poverty-stricken hag, but in some accounts this leads her to great spiritual realization.

77. The straw raincoat and broad bamboo hat are symbols of a poor wayfarer.

78. His poem is "It is precisely when / from time to time / the clouds hide the moon / that its beauty is enriched / and embellished" [*nakanaka ni / tokidoki kumo no / kakaru koso / tsuki o motenasu / kazashi narikeri*].

79. *Qi* (formerly written *ch'i*) is the Chinese notion of spiritual "breath" or vitality that all things have. The cultivation of pure, free-flowing *qi* is necessary for physical and spiritual health.

80. The area in which Edo (Tokyo) is located. Bashō has just returned there for the first time since he left for the Deep North in Third Month (May) of 1689.

81. An allusion to the *Zhuangzi*, where a small dove laughs at a phoenix, as a narrow-minded person laughs at the claims of a sage.

82. A reference to the journey of 1689 that resulted in *The Narrow Road to the Deep North*.

83. An allusion to a line in "Autumn Meditations," a collection of eight poems by Du Fu: "Again I greet chrysanthemum blossoms, shedding tears of nostalgia for the days of old."

84. *Fūryū.* See note 41, chapter 5, and the glossary.

85. *Hijiri*, originally a religious term denoting a shaman or ascetic with supernatural powers.

86. From a passage in Confucius's *Analects*, also quoted in Kenkō's *Essays in Idleness*.

87. Fujiwara Shunzei (1114–1204), great *waka* poet and critic, and father of Teika.
88. Accomplished *waka* poet and theorist (1180–1239) who commissioned the *Shinkokinshū*.
89. Actually it is the third of the five precepts.
90. The identity of this mountain is not known. Ki no Tsurayuki associated it with plum's scent and Kenkō quotes an unknown source saying "even in the dark of Kurabu Mountain there are many who are watching." The entire passage not only alludes frequently to *Essays in Idleness* but imitates the "personal essay" (*zuihitsu*) style of that work, and is similar to one of the short chapters from that book.
91. An epithet for a prostitute.
92. Zhuangzi was posthumously given the name True Man of the Southern Flower.
93. Two famous recluses. The scholar Sun Jing of the Three Kingdoms period locked himself in his room and read all night. The Song scholar Du Wulang is said to have remained in his locked house for thirty years.
94. Enomoto Tōjun was Kikaku's father, who died on the 29th day of Eighth Month (September 28, 1693).
95. If dust does gather, it must be a poor family that lacks food.
96. The Chrysanthemum Festival is traditionally celebrated on the 9th day of Ninth Month.
97. By Su Shi.
98. A Nō actor in Ōtsu and a *haikai* poet using the pen name Tan'ya.
99. This sentence refers to two stories from the *Zhuangzi*. In the first, Zhuangzi sees a skull and wonders mournfully of its fate, and then uses it as a pillow. In his sleep, the skull reproaches him for thinking that life is better than death, for the dead suffer no worries or injustices. The second story is the famous episode in which Zhuangzi wakes from dreaming that he was a butterfly, only to wonder if he is in fact a butterfly now dreaming he is Zhuangzi.

100. It is said that when the famous beauty and poet Ono no
     Komachi died, after becoming a poverty-stricken hag, mis-
     canthus plumes grew through her skull.
101. *Furu* means both "pass time" and "rain." Bashō's *hokku*
     draws on one by the *renga* master Sōgi: "In a world of rain
     / life is like a temporary shelter / from a wintry shower"
     [*yo ni furu mo / sarani shigure no / yadori kana*]. Note
     that there is a difference of only one word between Bashō's
     verse and Sōgi's.

GLOSSARY

bashō. "Banana" or "plantain." A small, tropical-looking tree with large oblong leaves that rarely bears fruit in Japan. The leaves tear easily in wind and rain, and so the plant has become a symbol of impermanence. Matsuo Bashō took his most famous pen name from this plant precisely because it was so vulnerable to nature elements and "useless." A seasonal word for autumn.

danrin. A popular school of *haikai* poetry established by Nishiyama Sōin (1605–1682). It gave poets greater freedom in subject matter, imagery, tone, and poetic composition than the earlier *Teimon* School. Bashō was a follower of this school before he set up his own, known as *Shōmon*.

fūga. "The poetic spirit." A combination of "wind" and "elegance," this term refers to the aesthetic vitality and sensitivity found in *haikai* poetry as well as associated arts such as *waka*, landscape painting, and the tea ceremony.

haibun. "Haikai prose-poems." Normally a brief prose text that exhibits *haikai* aesthetics and includes *hokku*. Bashō was the first great *haibun* writer.

haikai. "Comic, unorthodox." An abbreviation of *haikai no renga*, but also used as a general term for other genres and art forms that show *haikai no renga* aesthetics and what Bashō called the poetic spirit (*fūga*). In this general sense, it might be translated as Haikai Poetry or Haikai Art. For Bashō it involved a combination of both comic playfulness and spiritual depth, both ascetic practice and involvement in the "floating world" of human society.

haikai no renga. "Comic *renga*," although "unorthodox" or "plebian" may be more accurate than "comic." A verse form, similar to traditional *renga*, that developed in the late medieval and Tokugawa periods. Compared to traditional *renga*, its aesthetics were more inclusive in subject matter and imagery and more earthy and playful in tone. Parodies of the classical literature were common. Bashō was a master of *haikai no renga*.

haiku. An independent verse form with a 5–7–5 syllabic rhythm. A modern term, its was popularized by the great but short-lived poet Masaoka Shiki (1867–1902), who wanted to establish the *haiku* as a verse form that stands by itself, separate from the linked verses of a *renga*. It is supposed to contain a season word (*kigo*). When the West first learned about Bashō and other premodern poets, the term *haiku* was anachronistically applied to their *hokku*. Properly speaking, *haiku* refers only to poems written in the modern period (beginning 1868).

hokku. "Opening stanza." The first stanza of a *renga*, with a 5–7–5 syllabic rhythm. This stanza was considered the most important and was usually offered by the master poet at a linked-verse gathering. A season word was required. Eventually poets wrote *hokku* as semi-independent verse: as potential starting verses for a *renga* sequence, to accompany prose in travel journals and *haibun*, or to be admired on their own.

kigo. "Season word." A word that in the literary tradition suggests a particular season (e.g., autumn) and possibly a part of a season (e.g., early spring), even if the object (e.g., moon or bush warbler) may be seen in other seasons. Season words may be an image derived from human activity (such as a seasonal ritual) as well as from nature. Every *hokku* and *haiku* should contain a season word. Traditionally collections of Japanese *hokku* and *haiku* verse were organized by seasonal order. There are now numerous season words dictionaries (*saijiki* or *kigo jiten*).

kikō bungaku. "Travel literature." Accounts of travel in prose, often accompanied by verse. Similar to and overlapping *nikki bungaku,* diary literature.

monogatari. "Narrative." Prose narratives and tales, often including verse and sometimes quite lengthy. The genre began and reached its peak in the Heian Period (794–1186). The most famous is *The Tale of Genji* (*Genji monogatari*), by Murasaki Shikibu (ca. 1000).

mujō. "Impermanence." A prominent and complex idea in Japanese literature as well as Buddhism and Daoism, and central to Bashō's writings. One of the most fundamental aspects of life is its changefulness, which can take many forms: the regular cycles of the seasons, the creative transformations of nature, the rise and inevitable fall of ruling houses, the inescapable degeneration of aging, the inconstancy of lovers, the inevitability of death, the uncertainty of life, and so forth.

nikki bungaku. "Diary literature." Diaries have been a prominent form of high literature since the Heian Period (794–1186), although this term is fairly recent. See *kikō bungaku.*

renga. "Classical linked verse." *Renga* is a linked-verse or sequenced poem with multiple, alternating stanzas. The first stanza consists of a 5–7–5 syllabic rhythm. This is then coupled with another stanza with a 7–7 syllabic rhythm making a poetic unit of 5–7–5 and 7–7. Then comes the third stanza with a 5–7–5 rhythm. This is linked with the second stanza to make a poetic unit of 7–7 and 5–7–5, with the first stanza "forgotten." The linked verse continues this way, usually up to one hundred or, in Bashō's time, thirty-six stanzas (called a KASEN). Usually this was a group poem, with poets alternating stanzas. Modern *renga* is called *renku.*

sabi. "Loneliness." The term suggests both sorrowful and tranquil, a response to the realization and acceptance of the essential and shared loneliness of things. It can refer to an aspect of the fundamental nature of reality, a quality of a particular moment in nature, and the state of mind that apprehends and conforms to loneliness of the world. This term was a central spiritual-aesthetical ideal of Bashō's School.

utamakura. "Famous places." The term refers to places famous in Japanese history and culture. These had specific associations concerning historic events, famous people, aspects of nature, and emotional tone.

wabi. "Aesthetic rusticity." A complex term that suggest simplicity and poverty, unadorned natural beauty, the elegant patina of age, loneliness, freedom from worldly cares, refined aesthetic sensitivity, and tranquillity. In some cases, it includes a tone of deprivation and desolation.

BIBLIOGRAPHY

SELECTED EDITIONS OF BASHŌ'S LITERARY PROSE

Imoto Nōichi, et al., eds. *Matsuo Bashō shū*. Nihon koten bungaku zenshū. Vol. 41. Tokyo: Shogakkan, 1972.

——. *Bashō bunshū, Kyoraishō*. Nihon no koten. Vol. 55. Tokyo: Kadokawa Shoten, 1985.

——. *Bashō kushū*. Nihon no koten. Vol. 54. Tokyo: Kadokawa Shoten, 1984.

Komiya Toyotaka et al., eds. *Kōhon Bashō zenshū*. 10 Vols. Tokyo: Kadokawa Shoten, 1962–69.

Kon Eizō. *Bashō kushū*. Shinchō koten shūsei. Vol. 51. Tokyo: Shinchōsha, 1982.

Nakamura Shunjō. *Bashō Jiten*. Tokyo: Shunjūsha, 1978.

Ōiso Yoshio and Ōuchi Hatsuo, eds. *Shōmon hairon haibunshū*. Koten haibungaku taikei. Vol. 10. Tokyo: Shūeisha, 1970.

Ōtani Tokuzō and Nakamura Shunjō, eds. *Bashō kushū*. Nihon koten bungaku taikei. Vol. 45. Tokyo: Iwanami Shoten, 1962.

Sugiwara Shoichiro, et al., eds. *Bashō bunshū*. Nihon koten bungaku taikei. Vol. 46. Tokyo: Iwanami Shoten, 1959.

Toyama Susumu. *Bashō bunshū*. Shinchō koten shūsei. Vol. 17. Tokyo: Shinchōsha, 1978.

SELECTED TRANSLATIONS OF BASHŌ'S PROSE

Barnhill, David Landis, trans. *Bashō's Haiku: Selected Poems by Matsuo Bashō*. Albany: State University of New York Press, 2004.

Britton, Dorothy, trans. *A Haiku Journey*. Tokyo: Kodansha International, 1974.

Corman, Cid and Kamaike Susumu, trans. *Back Roads to Far Towns: Bashō's Oku-no-hosomichi*. 1980. Reprint, Hopewell, NJ: Ecco Press, 1996.

Hamill, Sam, trans. *The Essential Bashō*. Boston: Shambhala, 1999.

Keene, Donald, trans. *The Narrow Road to Oku*. Tokyo: Kodansha International, 1996.

Kerkham, Eleanor, trans. "Notes from the Traveler's Satchel." *The Tea Leaves* 2 (1965): 26–46.

McCullough, Helen Craig, ed. *Classical Japanese Prose: An Anthology*. Stanford, CA: Stanford University Press, 1990.

Miner, Earl, trans. *Japanese Poetic Diaries*. Berkeley, CA: The University of California Press, 1969.

Sato, Hiroaki, trans. *Bashō's Narrow Road; Spring and Autumn Passages*. Berkeley, CA: Stone Bridge, 1996.

Terasaki, Etsuko, trans. "The Saga Diary." *Literature East and West* 16 (1971–72): 701–718.

Ueda, Makoto, trans. *Bashō and His Interpreters: Selected Hokku with Commentary*. Stanford, CA: Stanford University Press, 1991.

Yuasa, Nobuyuki, trans. *The Narrow Road to the Deep North, and Other Travel Sketches*. Harmondsworth: Penguin, 1966.

Selected secondary sources

Barnhill, David. "Bashō as Bat: Wayfaring and Anti-Structure in the Journals of Matsuo Bashō (1644–1694)." *Journal of Asian Studies* 49 (May 1990): 274–290.

———. "Impermanence, Fate, and the Journey: Bashō and the Problem of Meaning." *Religion* 16 (1986): 323–341.

————. "Of Bashōs and Buddhisms." *Eastern Buddhist* 32.2 (fall 2000): 170–201.

————, ed. *At Home on the Earth: Becoming Native to our Place.* Berkeley, CA: University of California Press, 1999.

Elder, John. *Following the Brush: An American Encounter with Classical Japanese Culture.* Boston: Beacon Press, 1993.

Foard, James. "The Loneliness of Matsuo Bashō." In *The Biographical Process: Studies in the History and Psychology of Religion,* 363–391. The Hague: Mouton, 1976.

Keene, Donald. *Appreciations of Japanese Culture.* Tokyo: Kodansha, 1981.

————. *Travelers of a Hundred Ages.* New York: Henry Holt, 1989.

————. *World Within Walls: Japanese Literature of the Pre-Modern Era, 1600–1867.* New York: Grove Press, 1976.

LaFleur, William. *The Karma of Words: Buddhism and the Literary Arts in Medieval Japan.* Berkeley, CA: University of California Press, 1983.

Qiu, Peipei. *Adaptation and Transformation: Seventeenth Century Haikai and the Zhuangzi.* Honolulu: University of Hawaii Press, forthcoming.

Ross, Bruce, ed. *Journey to the Interior: American Versions of Haibun.* Rutland, VT: Tuttle, 1998.

Shirane, Haruo. *Traces of Dreams: Landscape, Cultural Memory, and the Poetry of Bashō.* Stanford, CA: Stanford University Press, 1998.

Shirane, Haruo, ed. *Early Modern Japanese Literature: An Anthology, 1600–1900.* New York: Columbia University Press, 2002.

Snyder, Gary. *The Back Country.* New York: New Directions, 1968.

Ueda, Makoto. *Matsuo Bashō.* 1970. Reprint, Tokyo: Kodansha International, 1982.

Watson, Burton, trans. *The Complete Works of Chuang Tzu.* New York: Columbia University Press, 1968.

INDEX

SELECTED NAMES, PLACES, AND THEMES

Abutsu, 9, 10, 30, 151n10
Ariwara Yukihira (Chūnagon),
   23, 41, 149n2, 154n38,
   154n44, 171n2
Asukai Masaaki, 31, 151n13

Benkei, 56, 160n50
Bo Juyi, 79, 97, 125, 131,
   163n97, 169n8, 171n1, 175n37
Bonchō (Nozawa Bonchō), 79,
   80, 81, 84, 169n9, 169n11,
   170n12
Buddha, 16, 34, 40, 46, 50, 51,
   55, 58, 62, 65, 70, 116, 123,
   125, 127, 130
Butchō, 53, 157n30
Chiri (Naemura Chiri), 1, 14, 16,
   147n1, 147n3

Corman, Cid, 11
Creative (zōka), 8, 29, 39, 61,
   114, 146n9, 151n7, 162n74

death, 1, 2, 6, 13, 16, 18, 33, 42,
   43, 45–46, 47, 49, 57, 59, 71,
   72, 77, 80, 85, 108, 111, 118,
   134, 141, 142

dream, 15, 22, 43, 62, 87, 88,
   98–99, 107, 128, 140, 142
Du Fu, 43, 94, 95, 97, 125,
   154n43, 163n83, 163n87,
   172n3, 172n6, 178n83
Du Mu, 15, 98, 147n4, 172n3

Elder, John, 11
Ehrlich, Gretel, 11
En no Gyōja, 157nn28–29
Etsujin (Ochi Etsujin), 45, 47,
   112, 151n15, 176n47

Fujiwara Kiyosuke, 159n39
Fujiwara Masatsune, 148n9
Fujiwara Shunzei, 139,
   179n87
Fujiwara Teika, 130
Fumikuni, 84, 85, 86

Genzui, 101
Go-toba, Emperor, 139,
   149n14
Gyōgi, 55, 116, 175n40

Hamada Chinseki, 122
Hamill, Sam, 11

Han Shan, 97, 172n13
heaven, 2, 6, 14, 36, 57, 60, 61,
  68, 70, 88, 98, 117, 119, 131,
  137, 138, 173n18
Huang Tingjian, 30, 85, 151n11

impermanence, 2, 4, 6, 13, 14,
  16, 17, 18, 25, 29, 33, 34, 39,
  40, 41, 42, 43, 45, 46, 49, 57,
  59, 60, 62, 63, 65, 70, 97, 98,
  110, 118, 122, 126, 131, 138,
  142
Ise, 15, 17, 32, 36, 70, 76, 77,
  103, 107, 121, 148n11,
  152n20, 168n159, 175n36

Jokushi (Nakagawa Jokushi), 61,
  101
Jōsō, 84, 85, 87, 170n12
journey, 5, 6, 13, 18, 19, 21, 22,
  23, 29, 30, 32, 33, 36, 37, 39,
  40, 41, 42, 45, 46, 49, 50, 57,
  59, 61, 64, 73, 77, 88, 96, 99,
  100, 102, 105, 113, 124, 126,
  134, 135, 136, 139

Kakei (Yamamoto Kakei), 45,
  112
Kamo no Chōmei, 9, 30,
  150n10, 151n10
Keene, Donald, 145n4, 146n8
Kikaku (Takarai Kikaku), 22, 30,
  85, 86, 97, 103, 141, 172n11,
  179n94
Ki no Tsurayuki, 9, 10, 30,
  151n10
Kūkai, 51, 108, 139, 153n30,
  169n6
Kyohaku, 58
Kyorai (Mukai Kyorai), 4, 79,
  80, 81, 82, 84, 87, 103, 129,
  169n11, 170n12
Kyoriku, 138–39

Li Bo, 97, 102, 152n23, 155n1,
  174n34
loneliness, 4, 25, 38, 43, 63, 65,
  73, 76, 82, 85, 93, 94, 95, 96,
  108, 121, 124, 126, 129, 142,
  143

Mangikumaru, 36, 37, 40
Mansei, 172n8
Matsushima, 5, 51, 58, 60, 61,
  68, 117, 126
Matthiessen, Peter, 11
Minamoto Toshiyori, 161n58
Minamoto Yorimasa, 158n38
Minamoto Yoshitomo, 17, 72,
  148n11
Minamoto Yoshitsune, 56,
  154nn40–41, 154n45, 160n50
Moritake (Arakida Moritake),
  17, 138, 148n11

Nara, 1, 20, 40, 41
Nijō Yoshimoto, 149n9
Nikkō, 50, 51, 52
Nōin, 58, 68, 114, 126, 158n37,
  160n55

Otokuni (Kawai Otokuni), 82,
  87, 170n17

past, 3, 5, 6, 13, 16, 34, 42, 43,
  49, 51, 53, 55, 56, 58, 59, 60,
  62, 64, 72, 80, 83, 116, 123,
  125, 129, 133, 137
purity, 17, 24, 38, 51, 54, 64, 65,
  66, 76, 86, 108, 109, 120,
  122, 124, 126

Ransetsu (Hattori Ransetsu), 24,
  83, 140n7

Saigyō, 8, 15, 17, 29, 39, 68, 74,
  82, 97, 107, 117, 130, 132,

139, 143, 147n5, 148n10,
152n26, 152n28, 153n34,
158n34, 159n42, 160n53,
167n146, 170nn12–14, 172n9,
173n16, 173n20, 174n33,
175n36, 177n71
Saitō Sanemori, 72, 166n129
Sanpū (Sugiyama Sanpū), 49, 61,
136, 155n3
Sarashina, 5, 45–48, 110–11
Sen no Rikyū, 8, 29, 122, 151n5
Senna (Mikami Senna), 88,
170n22
Sesshū, 8, 29, 150n5
Shirakawa, 49, 54, 55, 103, 114,
115, 126
Shirane, Haruo, 146n7
Shōhaku, 84, 88
Snyder, Gary, ix, 11,
Sodō (Yamaguchi Sodō), 105,
141, 162n76, 174n35
Sōgi, 8, 10, 29, 138, 143, 150n5
Sōha, 26, 82, 83
Sōkan (Yamazaki Sōkan), 122,
126, 138, 177n65
solitude, 4, 24, 32, 36, 38, 42,
43, 47, 55, 81, 82, 84, 87, 93,
94, 95, 96, 104, 110, 112,
116, 124, 125, 127, 134, 140,
141, 142
Sora (Iwanami Sora), 25, 26, 27,
50, 51, 62, 67, 69, 73, 89,
104, 115, 136, 149n3
sorrow, 13, 14, 24, 26, 30, 35,
36, 39, 40, 42, 43, 46, 47, 50,
56, 60, 63, 68, 70, 71, 72, 73,
80, 83, 86, 87, 88, 89, 94, 95,
96, 97, 99, 104–5, 107, 108,
110, 117, 119, 135, 137, 139,
141
Su Shi, 30, 94, 105, 143,
151n11, 164n97, 165n111,
177n66, 179n97

Taira no Kanemori, 158n35
Tao Qian, 100
Tao Yuanming, 134
Teishitsu (Yashuara Teishitsu),
23, 39, 149n1
Teitoku (Matsunaga Teitoku),
149n1
Tenyū, High Priest, 118
Tōjun, 141
Tokoku (Tsuboi Tokuku), 22,
151n14, 152n21
Tōzan, 136–37
tranquillity, 16, 24, 55, 64, 65,
79, 82, 87, 100, 103, 104,
106, 108, 122, 123, 129, 137,
140

Ukō, 80, 81, 169n11
Unchiku, 128
unreal, 50, 123–28

wabi, 4, 18, 80, 93, 94, 95, 122,
129
Wang Shiyu, 134
writing (literature), 8–11, 24, 29,
30, 43, 46, 51, 54, 61, 65, 67,
69, 73, 82, 84, 97, 98, 103,
105–6, 110, 112, 114, 116,
117, 125, 127–28, 134,
138–39, 141

Xi Shi, 69, 97, 173n17

Yoshida Kenkō, 153n35
Yoshino, 17, 30, 36, 39, 40, 89,
100, 148n9, 152nn23–24,
152nn27–28, 153n29
Yuasa, Nobuyuki, 11

Zhuangzi, 87, 101, 105, 142,
147n8, 173nn21–22, 173n24,
174n32, 177n72, 178n81,
179n92, 179n99